BIRTHS, DEATHS and MARRIAGES

from the
Platte City, Missouri

LANDMARK

August 18, 1875
to
December 31, 1877

Kari L. Montagriff

HERITAGE BOOKS
2009

HERITAGE BOOKS
AN IMPRINT OF HERITAGE BOOKS, INC.

Books, CDs, and more—Worldwide

For our listing of thousands of titles see our website
at
www.HeritageBooks.com

Published 2009 by
HERITAGE BOOKS, INC.
Publishing Division
100 Railroad Ave. #104
Westminster, Maryland 21157

Copyright © 2009 Kari L. Montagriff

All rights reserved. No part of this book may be reproduced or transmitted in any form or by any means, electronic or mechanical, including photocopying, recording or by any information storage and retrieval system without written permission from the author, except for the inclusion of brief quotations in a review.

International Standard Book Numbers
Paperbound: 978-0-7884-4941-3
Clothbound: 978-0-7884-8164-2

Table of Contents

INTRODUCTION TO THIS WORK iv

THE LANDMARK 1

NAME INDEX 118

Introduction to this work
Scope & Limitations of this Work

This work is a compilation of transcribed notices from the Platte City Landmark, Platte County, Missouri from September 1874-December 1877. It consists of entries of Births, Deaths, and Marriages.

Due to the Nature of these Old newspaper records, there are inevitably many entries, which have been missed. The Birth, Marriage and Death notices were interspersed with all the other notices of the day; there, being no set section in the newspaper into which these notices were placed. In addition, the researcher had to contend with the very nature of reading old microfilm; the fact that many words were illegible and some pages were missing, made this entire task very difficult.

These entries were taken from the Microfilm entitled: "Platte City Landmark August 18, 1875-December 1877", available from the State Historical Society of Missouri, Columbia, Mo.

"Definitions and Abbreviations:"

Instant or inst.=   The current month.
Last, or Ult. or Ultimo=   The month just preceding the current month.

Items in square brackets [___?___] are items which were not clear to the researcher, **OR** they denote the researchers personal remarks.

Ellipses (...) have been used where the announcement was very lengthy, so not included in its entirety.

Researcher Contact:
Kari Montagriff
P.O. Box 2081
Pagosa Springs, CO 81147
© 2003

The Landmark
Platte County Missouri

Friday September 18, 1874

Married:

At the residence of Hon E.H. **Norton** near Platte City, by Rev J. W. **Brown**, on the 15th inst., Mr. Proman **Blakley**, of Denver, Colorado, and Miss Ella **Moore**, of Platte City.

--At the residence of the officiating clergyman, in Weston, on the ---inst., by Rev J.Y. **Blakey**, Thos. B. **Rogers**, to Mrs. Venetia **Swearenger**, both of Platte County.

--At the same place and by the same, on the ___ inst., George **Vierheilig**, and Miss Mary E. **Wilson**, both of Weston.

--By the same at the M. E. Church South, on the 8th inst., George H. **Foote**, of Atchison, Kansas, to Miss Georgia E. **Parr**, of Weston.

Redman-Ashby:

In the M.E. Church South, Santa Rosa, on Sunday, August 30th, 1874, by Rev O.P. **Fitzgerald**, C.C. **Redman**, of Santa Rosa, and Miss Lizzie J. **Ashby**, of Heraldburg.

The marriage notice of C.C. **Redman** appears in an appropriate column. We cast after them (metaphorically) the old shoe of good luck. May their tribe increase. —*Sonoma, Cal. Democrat*

Killed:

We learn that on Wednesday of last week, Miss **Walters**, aged 28, daughter of Mr. **Walters** who lives near Camden Point, was killed by being thrown from a horse. We have not been able to obtain any particulars further than the horse was frightened by a passing railroad train which came across the public highway without the warning of bell or whistle.

Birth's, Death's and Marriages from the Platte City Missouri "Landmark"

Friday September 25, 1874

Married:

Gretna Green- There was a quiet little wedding at the office of the probate judge last Monday morning. Mr. Granville G. **Bailey** and Miss Eva **Lattin**, hailing from Leavenworth county Kansas presented themselves before his honor Judge **Chiles** and demanded to be made one flesh. The contracting parties having made satisfactory answers to the questions propounded to them, the judge speedily and gracefully pronounced the words that they evidently hankered after, and they departed as happy as two big sunflowers.

Friday October 2, 1874

The many friends of Mr. Rufus H. **Todd** will be surprised to learn that he is a benedict and has been for nearly a month. We do not know how he kept the affair so quiet, but he did it, and although the happy event occurred on the 8th day of September, we were none the wiser until yesterday. The fortunate lady is Miss Fannie **Davidson**, of Clay County, and Elder Joseph **Waller** the officiating clergyman. Ruf. and his fair bride are visiting the Fair and receiving congratulations at all hands.

Married:

J.**Beery** Esq., at the residence of the bride's father, Sept. 30. Israel **Boyd** to Mary E. **Galbraith**, both of this County.

At the M.E. church, South, in Linneus Mo, by Rev C. **Grimes**, Mr. J.P. **Bradley**, formerly of Platte county to Miss Mattie, daughter of S.D. **Sandusky**, Esq., all of Linneus, MO.

Although the announcement was late coming to hand, it is not too late, we hope, to extend the heartiest congratulations of THE LANDMARK to our old friend and subscriber and his estimable wife.

Birth's, Death's and Marriages from the Platte City Missouri "Landmark"

Friday October 16, 1874

Death of an Estimable Woman:

It becomes our painful duty to announce the death of Mrs. Martha Elizabeth **Adams**, the wife of Mr. Smith **Adams**, which sad event took place at the family residence, near Platte City on October 11th.

The deceased had long been suffering from a distressing disease, which, although all was done that human skill could do to relieve her, was sorely sapping the foundations of life. She was a most estimable woman and numbered as her friends and admirers all who knew her.

Mrs. **Adams** was born January 6th 1828. She became a member of the Baptist Church in 1853. She was married to Mr. Smith **Adams** on the 20th of January 1854. Her husband being a member of the Christian Church, she became a member of it in 1855, and from that time till death claimed her, she lived within its communion-a faithful, consistent, humble and devoted Christian.

The death of such a woman is at all times a social calamity, and the loss to the community wherein she lived is little less than that of her immediate family circle.

Connubial:

At the residence of Mr. And Mrs. Wm. **Chestnut**, five miles east of this city, on the evening of the 13th inst., by Elder J. W. **Waller** of Liberty, Mr. W. P. **Jones** of St. Joseph, to Miss Della L. **Chestnut** of this county.

The attendants were, Mr. P.E. **Chestnut** of St. Joe and Miss Lida **Park** of Platte City. The following ladies and gentleman accompanied the bridal party on their tour: Mr. Malin **Lewis** and Miss Katie **Lewis** of Jimtown; Miss Fanute **Breckenridge**, Mr. Huston **Miller**, Mr. Prettie Ellie **Chestnut**, Miss Katie **Payne** and Mr. Hugh **Miller** of St. Joe, and Mr. Frank **Jones** of Council Bluffs.

Friday October 16, 1874 (Continued)

Married:

On Sunday, Oct., the 13th, Mr. Nathaniel **Wilkinson**, of this city to Miss Lydia **Phelps**, of Allen county, Kansas.

Mr. **Wilkinson** is one of the most industrious young men in the county, and all the old Benedicts should give him all the encouragement possible, we bespeak for Mr. W. a bright and happy future. May his undertakings in the future be as successful as those of the past.

Friday October 23, 1874

Married:

On the 15th inst. By Elder J.W. **Brown**, at the residence of the bride's parents, David E. **Pendleton**, Esq., formerly of Kentucky to Miss Anna, daughter of Bluford **Adkins**, Esq. of this county.

May prosperity and happiness attend them.

Gone Home:

William **Ridenbaugh**, the founder of the St. Joseph *Gazette*, and one of the early pioneers of the metropolis of the Missouri Valley, departed this life suddenly on Sabbath last at twenty five minutes past two o'clock. Apoplexy took him off in the prime of life. He was one of the first and best citizens of St. Joseph, and his many friends throughout the State, will morn his demise.

Birth's, Death's and Marriages from the Platte City Missouri "Landmark"

Friday October 30, 1874

Married:

At the residence of the bride's mother, Oct 22, 1874 by Rev F.P. **Foreman** of Liberty, Mr. David R. **Edwards**, merchant of Liberty, to Miss Mollie **Cary**, daughter of Mrs. May A. **Cary**, of Platte Co MO.

Friday November 6, 1874

Married:

At the residence of the bride's father, Mr. Wm. **Couch**, by Elder Joseph W. **Waller**, October 29th, 1874, Inst, Dr. J.C. **Rogers** at Lee's Summit, to Miss Dora M **Couch**, of Platte county.

The bride is one of the fairest and most accomplished daughters of old Platte. She is a graduate of Christian College and has had all the advantages which the pride of parents and friends, wealth and social position can give. Added to all these are her incomparable graces of person and amiability of disposition. Her husband is a stranger to us, but we trust that he is worthy of the jewel he has won, and to both we tender our congratulations and best wishes for their future happiness.

Friday November 13, 1874

Died:

At the residence of his father near Weston, on Sunday, Nov 8th, of Typhoid fever, Mr. Harvey **Owens**, son of Mr. Madison **Owens**, aged about thirty years.

Birth's, Death's and Marriages from the Platte City Missouri "Landmark"

Friday November 13, 1874 (Continued)

Married:

On the 5th inst, by Elder Wm. H. **Thomas**, at the residence of the bride's parents, in this county, Capt M.L. **Todd** to Mrs. Nannie **Anderson**, daughter of Mr. J.C. **Bywaters**, all of this county. THE LANDMARK tenders its congratulations to Captain **Todd** and his charming bride.

Obituary:

Died of congestion of the brain, at the family residence, at East Leavenworth, on the 30th ultimo, George H. **Banning**, eldest son of Cole L and Huldah A. **Banning**, in the nineteenth year of his age.

The lamented Henry was known by all his associates to be a young man of unsurpassed moral and social worth, whose delight was to render comfort and happiness to all around him.

During the past few years he had been engaged in the mercantile business, and in this occupation, by fair dealing, and gentlemanly deportment, he seems to have secured the entire confidence of his many customers, and thus has succeeded in establishing a reputation for honor, which will live long after the tall grass shall have waved over his head.

He has gone down to the grave, honored for his virtues and lamented by his numerous friends and acquaintances, many of whom are heard to express their sympathy for the sorely bereaved parents, whose fond hopes have been blasted, and whose hearts have been almost crushed in consequence of this mighty work of death; doomed as they are to pass through this same ordeal, to which, until recently, they were comparatively strangers.

May they be sustained in this, the deepest sorrow, by grace Divine, and may their loss be Henry's gain.

Birth's, Death's and Marriages from the Platte City Missouri "Landmark"

Friday November 20, 1874

Died:

At the residence of the parents in Platte City of croup on the 18th inst, Henry, son of Henry and Jane **Lanzer**, aged two years and 5 months.

Married:

We are requested to notice the marriage of Dr. Loren **Sweeney** to Miss. Georgie M. **Robinson**-both of Jackson County- at Hickmans Mills, on the 11th inst.

Friday November 27, 1874

Married:

At the residence of the bride's parents, by Elder J. B. **McClary**, on the 24th inst., Mr. A. J. **Coleman** to Miss Myra **Collins**, daughter of John **Collins** of this City...

Friday December 4, 1874

Died:

On the morning of the 28th of November, James **Harvel**, infant son of Mr. & Mrs. James **Harvel**, aged about 6 months.

Friday December 4, 1874 (Continued)

Married:

On the morning of November 22, 1874 at the residence of the bride's father, one mile and a half south of Newark, Knox County, Mo by Rev J.H. **Poland**, Dr. Jim **Holt** of Platte Mo and Mrs. Georgia A **Porter**.

Died:

We regret to learn of the death of Elma Ber the infant son of Cyrus P. and Mary **Gilbert** in Weston on Saturday night at 10 o'clock, aged three and a half months. This was the only son of the devoted parents and we know well their sorrow in the hour of their sad bereavement and extend to them our condolence over the loss of their little babe.

Friday December 11, 1874

Married:

--At the residence of Mrs. Lucy **Todd**, by Elder J.W. **Brown** on the 7th inst, Mr. A.H. **Todd** to Miss Sudie **Morgan**.

We are glad to welcome friend "Hatch" to the society of Benedicts. THE LANDMARK extends its congratulations to him on securing so estimable partner for life's journey. May the skies above the happy pair, who have thus commenced a new life so auspiciously, never be less bright than now.

Married:

--At the residence of the bride, by Elder J.W. **Brown**, on the 9th inst. Mr. J.C. **Sutherland** to Miss Alice **Johnson**, daughter of the late Capt. R.D. **Johnson**.

We congratulate Mr. **Sutherland** in securing on of Platte County's fairest, and most accomplished daughters. May a clear bright sky above them, flowery paths beneath them and found recollections of the past ever be theirs.

Friday December 11, 1874 (Continued)

Married:

--At the residence of Jackson **Bradley** by Esquire Jeremiah **Berry**, on the 6th inst, Mr. James **Lawerence** to Miss Florence **Bradley**, all of this county.

THE LANDMARK acknowledges the receipt of a goodly quantity of cake, and extends a hearty congratulation to the happy couples. We advise those contemplating matrimony, and wishing to be joined indissolubly, to call upon Esq. **Beery**, for he knows how to do it.

Friday December 18, 1874

Died:

Mr. Samuel **Langley**, a well-known citizen of Lee Township, died on Sunday last, after a protracted illness.

Death of Mrs. Clemings:

Mrs. Charlotte T. **Clemings**, wife of our esteemed fellow citizen, Mr. G. F. **Clemings**, died at the family residence in Platte City, Dec. 12th. Mrs. **Clemings** was the daughter of John and Elizabeth **Kuykendall**, and was born in Lincoln County, Kentucky, July 26th, 1828. She removed with her parents to Clay County, Missouri, in September 1835, and thence to Platte County, in December 1838.

She became a member of the Christian Church in 1815, and from that time to the day of her death lived in the communion of that church, a sincere, devoted and practical Christian. On the 18th of January, 1852 she was married to Mr. G. F. **Clemings**. The fruits of this union were six children, three of whom are living—two daughters and one son.

Mrs. **Clemings** had been in poor health for many months, and was therefore unable to with stand the severe attack of pneumonia, which resulted in her death.

Her funeral was preached by Elder J. H. **McClary** who made eloquent and touching allusion to the many noble qualities and shining virtues of the deceased.

In every relation of life she was a most estimable women and her place in society, which she adorned, will not soon be filled.

Birth's, Death's and Marriages from the Platte City Missouri "Landmark"

Friday December 18, 1874 (Continued)

Died:

Capt James **McCord**, who died in St. Louis on the 25th of last month had many friends and relatives in Platte. He was related to Mr. James **Wallace** and Mrs. **Nash**, of this county, and only a few months ago was with them on a visit. He was a man of estimable qualities of heart and mind.

Friday December 25, 1874

Married:

December 22, 1874 by Elder J. W. **Brown**, Thomas J. **Cole** to Miss Rosa **Lewis**, all of Platte County. May prosperity and happiness attend them through life.

Married:

On Wednesday last, the 23 inst at 10 o'clock AM at the residence of the bride's parents by Elder J. B. **McClary** of Leavenworth. Allen R. **Hall** Esq., of Clay County to Miss Dora, daughter of Dr. F.M. **Johnson** of this city...

Friday January 1, 1875

Married:

At the residence of the bride's parents near Ridgley, Platte County, Mo., by Elder J.B. **McClary** of Leavenworth on Wednesday Dec. 23 1874, Mr. William **Black** to Miss Bell **Beery**, dau of John A. **Beery**, Esq., all of Platte.

Birth's, Death's and Marriages from the Platte City Missouri "Landmark"

Friday January 1, 1875 (Continued)

A large number of the friends of the young couple were present and witnessed the nuptials. They embark upon their married life full of hope and promise and cheered by the best wishes of their numerous friends everywhere.

Death of Mrs. Kirtley:

We learn with feelings of regret of the death of Mrs. Sue E. **Kirtley**, wife of Mr. Phillip **Kirtley**. She died at the residence of her husband, near Golden City, Colorado, on the 23rd of December, of consumption. She was the daughter of Mr. Milton **Darnall**, a former well known citizen of Platte County, and a sister of Mr. R. T. **Darnall**, Treasurer of Platte County. She was about twenty-five years old. About two years ago she went to Colorado with her husband and her fathers family in the vain effort to check the encroachments of the insidious disease that had seized upon her. For a while she apparently improved but the treacherous disease had too firm a hold upon her and the melancholy result is now announced. She was highly educated and possessed of those domestic qualities that made her exceptional women. She leaves two young children to mourn her loss, besides her husband, parents, and brothers and sisters. May she rest peacefully in her Western grave until the final resurrection.

Died:

On the night of the 29th inst., of croup, Gertie, only daughter of T. L. and Belle **Hon**, aged about three years

January 29, 1875

Wm. Allen:

Aged about thirty-two, died at his residence in Clinton County, on Sunday of last week. He was a son-in-law of Mr. W.D. **Bonnel** of Platte city.

January 29, 1875 (Continued)

Sad:

Last week a little child of Mr. James H. **Littlejohn** was fatally burned. The little fellow, about two years old, lighted a paper which came in contact with its clothing and it was soon burned so badly that all efforts to save its life were futile. The funeral took place at Platte City on Monday. Our heart felt sympathies are extended to the parents of the unfortunate child.

An Old Citizen Gone:

Owing to our absence last week, the notice of the death of Mr. A. W. **Hughes** was omitted. Mr. A. W. **Hughes** died on the 11 inst, at his home in Wyandotte County, Kansas, in the sixty-third year of his age. He was buried at the Green burying ground near Farley on Wednesday January 15th. Mr. **Hughes** was an old and well-known citizen of this county and leaves many friends and relatives among us to mourn his loss. He was an upright and honorable man and a useful citizen.

Friday February 5, 1875

Married:

--At the residence of Mr. [Coon?] **Hunt**, in Platte City, by Esquire Jeramiah **Beery**, on the 3rd inst, Mr. Alex. **Smith** and Miss Pheule **Hunt**, daughter of the late Charles **Hunt**.

Married:

At the residence of the bride's parents on Thursday evening, the 28th ult. By Elder Joseph **Waller**, Mr. D. A. **Chance** to Miss Lizzie, daughter of G.W. and N. A. **Thompson**, all of Platte County.

Attendants: Robt. **Thompson** and Miss Ida **Wilson,** G. B. **Spratt** and Miss Willie **Murray**.

Birth's, Death's and Marriages from the Platte City Missouri "Landmark"

Friday February 5, 1875 (Continued)

After the ceremony was over, the numerous friends and acquaintances attendance, partook of a magnificent repast prepared for the occasion. May they go through life with an eye on the main Chance, blessed with prosperity and plenty.

Passing Away:

The pioneers of this community rapidly passing away. Nearly every week we are called upon to chronicle the death of one or more. This week the number is three.

--Mr. Preston **Whitlock** died of consumption on the 24th ult. He lived near Smithville, and was a good citizen, husband and father. We did not learn his age.

--Mr. William **DeBeery** of the same neighborhood, died of pneumonia on the 27th ult. The round of his years was complete having passed the scriptural three score and ten.

--Mr. John **Shortridge** died of typhoid fever at his residence two miles west of Camden Point, on the 29th ult. Mr. **Shortridge** was sixty-three years old and had been a resident of Platte County for Thirty-five years. He was a member of the Christian Church and illustrated the principles he professed in his every days walk and conversation.

Friday, February 12, 1875

Deaths:

The following deaths of citizens of this county have been reported to us since our last issue:

--Mrs. Margaret **Fulton** died on the 3d inst. She was born in East Tennessee, June 1st 1793, and came to Platte in 1838, her husband, William **Fulton**, died in 1870. Mrs. **Fulton** was one of the oldest residents of the county. She was one of that class of noble women which is too rapidly passing away.

Birth's, Death's and Marriages from the Platte City Missouri "Landmark"

Friday, February 12, 1875 (Continued)

--Thomas **Alvis**, an old and well known citizen of this county, died at his residence in Magie Township on the 4th inst., after a protracted illness.

--Lee **Hamilton** died at the residence of his brother Samuel **Hamilton**, near Camden Point, on the 5th inst., of pneumonia, He was a young man of fine promise, and his death is great lamented.

Died:

At the residence of Price **Starks** near Weston, Platte county, Mo., on Wednesday, the 3d day of February, 1875, Mrs. Eleanor L. **Morton**, in the eighty-third year of her age. Mrs. **Morton** was the widow of Richard **Morton**, an eminent minister of the Baptist church of Clark, co, Ky., many years ago, and was the mother of Elder Richard **Morton** of that county, and of Dr. J.F. **Morton**, Mrs. Isaac O. **Parish** and Mrs. Price **Starks** of Platte County, Mo. She died as she lived, a devoted and consistent Christian.

Died:

Miss Lizzie **Cockrill**, daughter of Mr. Clinton **Cockrill**, died on the 10th inst., after a protracted illness. Funeral from the family residence at 12 o'clock to-day (Friday.)

Married:

At the residence of the bride's parents in Platte City, Mo., by Rev. J. W. **Brown,** on the 9th inst., Mr. Amos G. **Marshall** to Miss Mary E. **Brady**.

A select party of friends and relatives witnesses the interesting ceremony and extended to them a hearty *bon voyage* on their journey through life. THE LANDMARK extends its congratulations and wishes them all the happiness accorded to mortals here below.

Birth's, Death's and Marriages from the Platte City Missouri "Landmark"

Friday, February 19, 1875

Died:

Gen. Chester **Harding**, well known in these parts as a Federal Brigadier General during the war, died in St. Louis on the 10th inst.

Died:

Mr. Felix **Pendleton** died of pneumonia at the residence of his brother, near Second Creek church, last Friday morning. He was unmarried and about thirty years old. He was buried by the Odd Fellows, of which order he was a member.

Married:

At the residence of the bride's parents in Platte City, Mo., by Rev H.W. **Currin** on February 17, 1875, Mr. Richard **Mayo**, of Clinton county, Missouri, to Miss Laura **Mason**, daughter of R. F. **Mason**.

Mr. **Mayo** is not an entire stranger to us and is recognized as a gentleman in the full sense and true meaning of that much abused word; yet, just how he has succeeded in invading our little social circle and robbing it of one of its brightest and loveliest jewels, passes our comprehension; but so it is, and what is our loss is most certainly his gain. One of the sweetest and most amiable of all our fair girls, we sincerely wish the measure of her happiness may be complete and her life be one long summer day of love.

Married:

--On the 11th inst, at the residence of the bride's mother, by Elder W. H. **Williams**, Mr. Fountain **Waller** to Miss Mary **Johnston**, all of this county.

It was a quiet little affair, only the relatives and a few intimate friends being present, yet the nuptials were auspicious of long lives of happiness and prosperity. In all the aracana of the future THE LANDMARK hopes they may find nothing but the full fruition of their fervent love.

Birth's, Death's and Marriages from the Platte City Missouri "Landmark"

Friday, February 26, 1875

Death of a Prominent Citizen:

Mr. Charles W. **Pullins**, a prominent citizen of this county, died at his residence, near Camden Point, on Thursday morning of last week. About one week before he was attacked by a violent chill which was merely the precursor of the pneumonia, a disease at this time fearfully prevalent throughout the county. Occasionally he would rally and reports would reach us to the effect that he was recovering, but all such appearances were deceptive. Mr. **Pullins** was the son of Mr. William **Pullins** and was born in Madison county, Kentucky, and removed to Platte county in 1857. He was a conscientious, upright, honorable citizen, and in his death, in the vigor of his manhood, the community has sustained a severe loss.

Death of Mrs. Perrin:

Mrs. Mary **Perrin**, wife of Wm F. **Perrin**, one of the most prominent citizens of Camden Township, died at the residence of her husband, near Camden Point, on Sunday, Feb. 21st, 1875. She died of pneumonia after an illness of a few days. Mrs. **Perrin** was one of the purest, truest and most amiable women in Platte County, and was a shining light in the elegant and refined society in which she moved. She was an earnest, consistent Christian woman, respected by all and beloved by those who knew her best. No greater calamity could befall the neighborhood than the one it is now forced to sustain in the death of Mrs. **Perrin**.

Death of Brother Felix Pendleton:

It becomes our sad duty to announce to the brothers of Missouri and Kentucky, the death of the above brother, who departed this life Friday, February 12th, 1875. Brother **Pendleton** had been suffering with Pneumonia for ten days, when nature would no longer sustain him death was the inevitable result. His funeral was preached at Second-creek church by Brothers **Devlin** and **Waller**. His remains were conducted to the cemetery by the brothers of Gosneyville and Smithville lodges and then interred by them with the honors of the I.O.O.F.

Resolved, That while the brotherhood throughout the states if Missouri and Kentucky mourns the sudden death, we as his brothers appreciate keenly his loss. In his death we are deprived of an earnest, faithful, and intelligent worker, ever ready to serve where labor was to be performed. Possessed of a kind, sympathetic and charitable disposition, he commanded the respect and won the affections of all who knew him.

Birth's, Death's and Marriages from the Platte City Missouri "Landmark"

Friday, February 26, 1875 (Continued)

Felix Pendleton--

Resolved, That we tender to the family and aged mother of the deceased, our heartfelt sympathy in this their hour of deep affliction.

Resolved, that our lodge-room emblems and charter be draped in mourning for the space of thirty days.

Resolved, That a copy of these resolutions be sent to the family and mother of our late Brother under seal and also to the *Advance*, published in Liberty, Mo.

W.F. **Nelson**

A. T. **Douglas**

John [G__?__]   Committee

Friday, March 5, 1875

Married:

On the evening of the 3d inst. At the residence of the widow **Todd's** by the Rev. J. W. **Brown**, Mr. Joseph **Akers** to Miss Eliza **Todd**, all of Platte County.

Died:

On the 1st inst., at her residence, south of Platte City, at an advanced age, Mrs. Patsy **Kimsey**, wife of the late Thomas **Kimsey**, and mother of Mr. Wade H. **Kimsey**, of Miller Township, aged about 80 years.

Died:

On Saturday the 27th ult., Miss Emm, daughter of John **Miller**, Esq., near Camden Point, aged 16 years. She died of consumption and was greatly beloved by all who knew her.

Birth's, Death's and Marriages from the Platte City Missouri "Landmark"

Friday, March 5, 1875

Died:

On Saturday the 27th ult., William **Clay**, of Camden Point, aged 79 years. Mr. **Clay** died in Leavenworth of pneumonia where he had gone for treatment. Mr. **Clay** was one of the oldest citizens of Platte County.

With The Angels:

Died on the 2d inst. At 2 o'clock a.m. in this city, Cara E., only child of W.F. and Helen C. **Cockrill**, aged eighteen months. Another bud plucked from the parents tem; another jewel added to the throng of the little angelic ones, radiant in eternal light. [Tribute not copied]

Died:

On Sunday the 28th, ult., in Tracy, Mrs Catherine, wife of Mr. John **Ryan**, aged 40 years. Mrs. **Ryan** was born in Kilrush, county Clare, Ireland. She had resided in Missouri since 1870. She leaves a stricken husband and an only child, a son twenty one years of age. She was a devoted wife and mother, and all sympathize with the bereaved ones in this sad hour of their calamity. Her remains were interred at Mount Calvery Catholic cemetery, Leavenworth Kansas.

New Orleans Picayune and Brownsville, Texas papers, please copy.

Sudden Death:

We learn with regret of the sudden death of Mrs. **McCall** at Union Mills, in this county on the evening of the [24th] ult. Mrs. **McCall** was aged about 25 years, she was attending to her household duties but a few hours before her death. Her sudden death leaves a desolate family of a devoted husband and two children, the latter aged, one of them two years and the other about four months.

Birth's, Death's and Marriages from the Platte City Missouri "Landmark"

Friday, March 12, 1875

Waldron Items-March 8th 1875

Our quiet neighborhood was suddenly aroused on the 4th, by a very sudden freak of matrimony. The happy couple were Mr. Northcut Washington **Naylor** and Miss Hannah Malinda **Kearnes**, of the township. They were married by the Rev. Mr. **Avery**, of Jackson County, and assisted by Rev. **Renfro** of Wyandotte, Kan. The many friends of both parties were present, and the sumptuous dinner that was prepared made all things pass off quite lively, and the jokes that were passed were many and in good spirits. Miss **Kearnes** was one of our most accomplished young ladies just in her sweet sixteenth year, and Mr. **Naylor** a widower of fifty-two years of age, but as young apparently as a boy of eighteen. Everything passed off quite pleasantly until the mischievous passions of two of the neighbors were set to work. They were A. **Miller** and R.S. **Weldon**. They thought they would give the couple an old fashioned charivari. So at about eight o'clock in the evening, they procured three fine large bells, and advanced within about one hundred yards of the premises, where Mr. M. halted with the bells, and Mr. W. advanced to the house and when within a few yards of the house he gave a yell that resounded for miles and Mr. M. commenced the most hideous rattling of bells that has ever been heard in this county. It soon brought the inmates of the house to the door, and there stood Mr. W. ready to inquire for Mr. **Naylor**, he being called upon advanced to the door and inquired of Mr. W. what was wanted. O! what a fib he told!

Mr. W. stated to him that there was about fifty in the crowd where the bells were and they had chosen his as their leader, and that they requested him to come to the house and see if they were prepared to receive them. Mr. **Naylor** thought that his time had come, and told Mr. W. that he would give him ten dollars of he would be so kind as to check the crowd, and told Mr. W. to go and get one of his horses and go to Parkville or Waldron and get the boys what they wanted to drink. Mr. W. agreed to do so and left the house and went back where he had left his partner, Mr. M. who was still at his post ringing his bells, and told him of his success, when they both gave three hearty cheers and departed for their homes, to spend the rest of the night in thinking how nicely the had sold Mr. **Naylor**.

For fear that I worry your readers, I will postpone giving you all the details this week, but will keep you posted for a few weeks to come in regard to the wedding.

Friday, March 12, 1875 (Continued)

Died:

On the 6th inst at 4 o'clock A.M. near Platte City, Mrs. Mattie **Park**, wife of Mr. Simpson **Park**, aged 46 years.

Mrs. **Park** was born in Clay County, Mo. She was the daughter of Mr. John R. **Peters**. Mrs. Park was a woman of fine intelligence and considerable cultivation, endowed by nature with great energy and good judgment. She resolutely persisted in whatever she believed to be right, and could not be induced under any circumstances to compromise with what she believed to be wrong. In religion, she was a Christian and a member of the Scottish Kirk in an early day, when they observed the letter of the law. As a neighbor, she was ever ready to discharge her duty, and all around her will hear testimony to her usefulness in time of sickness and distress. As a friend, she was as true and steadfast as the grand moral principles upon which her faith was founded.

Throughout her protracted illness, she never murmured or repined at her fate; and retaining all her faculties unimpaired to the last, met with death with the same courage with which she had encountered the trials of life. Though wasted and enfeebled in body to the last degree, her faith never faltered, and she left this earth in the hope of a bright and glorious future.

Friday, March 19, 1875

Obituary:

Miss Julia **Brooks**, daughter of John and Julia **Brooks** of Clay Co., Mo, was born Feb 16th, 1860. On March 11th 1875, she bade us farewell at the Mo. Female School, to enter that school above, where she will no longer need our instruction, but where she will sit at the feet of the Great Master himself. She came among us about five weeks since, and almost immediately after her arrival was taken sick with pneumonia.

Although a stranger, she was not treated as such, and all that Physicians and kind friends could do was most cheerfully done.

Her father, who was with her frequently during her sickness, was present when she so tranquilly yielded up her spirit.

She died, trusting in that Savior, to whom she more than two years ago, consecrated her brief life.

Friday, March 19, 1875 (Continued)

Married:

At the residence of the bride's father, Mr. James **Tate**, on the [11th] of March, Marcus Aurelus **Cox**, to Miss Jennie **Tate**. THE LANDMARK was remembered and complimented, and it is the wish that [_?_] may have no thorns, no rugged ways, no clouds to diminish the peace and happiness of these whom "God had just joined together." May our friend never fail to maintain the good name and fame of his patronymic, but for the world is better off because it has been blessed with Cox.

Obituary:

It has pleased the Great Creator in his all wise providence, to take from our midst our worthy and much beloved brother Wm. **Clay**, whose kind and gentle spirit took its flight on the night of the 27th of February, while Christ held the lamp to light it into the port of glory.

He was one of the first settlers of Platte County, but a few days more he would have been 75 years old. He was married at about the age of 25 to Sarah **Collet**, daughter of Abraham **Collet**, with whom he lived very happily until a few years since, she was separated from him by death. They had born unto them eleven children, ten of whom are still living. He was a kind and affectionate father. When he started in life, he had but little of this world's goods, but by industry and strict economy, he accumulated sufficient to live comfortably and give his children a liberal education.

The deceased was a member of the Baptist Church for nearly fifty years, and continued in it as one of its most exemplary members until the Lord called him home to rest from his Labors, and enjoy his reward.

He was truly among the excellent of earth. Ten such persons would have saved Sodom from it's ill-fated destruction, and ut for such now on earth, none would remain to record the sad fate of this world. If brother **Clay** had an enemy among all his acquaintances we have failed to find it out.

The proclamation from Heaven has said for the consolation of his friends, and all others, "Write, blessed are the dead who die in the Lord, for they shall rest from their labors and their works do follow them." The spirit has said, "Yes, write it" this surpasses all epitaphs and superscriptions written by men, as far as heaven passes earth. Yes, brother **Clay** now rests from his labors. Trouble, toil and pain will never more disturb his noble heart. [Tribute & Resolutions follow, but not included here]

Birth's, Death's and Marriages from the Platte City Missouri "Landmark"

Friday, March 26, 1875

Married:

At the residence of the bride's father by Eld. W. H. **Williams**, Mr. Lee M. **Darnell**, of Platte City to Miss Nannie **Hon**, on Thursday, March 18, 1875.

Also:

On the 23rd last, at the residence of the bride's parents at Leavenworth city by Elder J.B. **McCleery**, Bam **Evans**, Esq., to Miss Josie **Darley**, all of Leavenworth.

Friday, April 2, 1875

Death of George W. Crobarger

Mr. Geo. W. **Crobarger**, one of the oldest and most respected citizens of Platte County died at his residence near Platte city March 25th. He was born in Virginia, March 22, 1808, and was therefore sixty-five years old at the time of his death. For a great many years he had been a resident of this county and was honored and respected by all who knew him. He was a strict member of the Methodist church, South, and died as he lived- a Christian. He leaves a family and a large number of relatives to revere his memory and emulate the example of his life.

Married:

At the residence of the bride's mother, near Platte city by Rev. J.M. **Brown**, on March 21st, Mr. William **Hart** to Miss Paulina **Stewart**, all of Platte County.

We congratulate our excellent friends and trust for them life will be all sunshine, and that prosperity may ever attend them.

Birth's, Death's and Marriages from the Platte City Missouri "Landmark"

Friday, April 9, 1875

Death of a Veteran:

Mr. Samuel **Hodges** died at his residence near Second Creek church, on the 4th inst in the eighty-sixth year of his age. He was a soldier in the war of 1812 and his fund of anecdote and reminiscence of those sterling times was in exhaustible. He was a man of great intelligence and sterling integrity revered by his numerous programs and beloved by all who knew him. With honor untarnished and the record of a long life unsullied he sleeps well the sleep that knows no waking.

Friday, April 16, 1875

Married:

--On the 7th inst. by Elder B. **Waller**, at the residence of the bride's parents, Mr. Geo. W. **Chinn** to Miss Sallie **Robertson**, daughter of Robert I. **Robertson**, all of this county.

If our wishes could add anything to the already overflowing cup of happiness which our friend **Chinn** has qualified, his skies would be all sunshine; his paths strewn with roses; his mornings brimful with the glory of Aurora, his evenings resplendent with the hopes of Diana, and all his life an Eden and a foretaste of Heaven.

April 23, 1875

Death of Mr. Snail:

It becomes our painful duty to chronicle the death of another of the oldest and best citizens of this part of the State. The lengthening line still stretches out, and the record becomes eloquent with the names of those who have crossed over to the other side, leaving to us only the memory of their virtues and the history of their well-spent lives.

April 23, 1875 (Continued)

On Wednesday of last week news reached us that Dr. James B. **Snail**, of Smithville, had been stricken down with apoplexy. He had been visiting a patient and complaining of feeling unwell, returned to his residence and laid down. In less that an hour he was speechless and apparently unconscious. The best medical skill was immediately summoned, and was prompt in attendance, but unfortunately it was unavailing. Dr. **Snail** lingered until two o'clock p.m. Thursday, when he quietly and peacefully breathed his last, surrounded by his family and a host of friends to whom he had endeared himself by a life-time of devotion and unselfish interest.

He was born in Clark County, Kentucky, in 1821 or 1822. With his parents he removed to Smithville, Clay County, Missouri in 1849, where he has ever since resided in the active practice of the profession of medicine and surgery. He was a man of fine personal appearance and was generous and magnanimous to a fault. His splendid social qualities made him a marked man in any assembly, possessing, as he did, all the grace of through education and extensive reading. As a physician he had few equals in skill and experience and loved his profession because it gave him the power to confer blessings upon the unfortunate and suffering. As a husband and father he was a model worth of emulation, and as a neighbor, the affection of the entire neighborhood were entwined about him. During the Mexican War he was a surgeon in the United States army and there illustrated the virtues which found fuller recognition afterwards.

He was quietly laid to rest beside the remains of his father and mother in the old family burying ground near Judge **Brasfield's** in this county, last Friday, A large number of his old neighbors and friends gently and reverently performed the sad rites of sepiture. A great and good man has fallen.

Married:

At the residence of Mr. Sidney **Lanter**, in Farley, Platte County, Mo., by Elder Richard **Thomas**, on the 18th inst., Mr. Charles **Hardesty**, of Las Animas, Colorado, to Miss Carrie **Sutton**, of Platte county.

April 30, 1875

Death of Mrs. Charlotte Jenkins of the oldest residents of our town and county has passed away and again our people are in mourning. We allude to the death of Mrs. Charlotte **Jenkins**, relict of the late Howel **Jenkins**, who died at the residence of her son, Mr. Thomas E. **Jenkins**, In Platte City, on Saturday, April 24th, 1875, after a very brief and comparatively painless illness.

Mrs. **Jenkins** was born in Merthyr Tydvil, Wales, on the 14th of January 1814. She was married to Howel **Jenkins** June 30th 1838, and with her husband emigrated to America in 1840, settling in Platte City the same year, where they ever afterwards resided. Of this union six children were born—four sons and two daughters—only two of whom survive, our respected citizens, Messrs. Thomas E. and William T. **Jenkins**. Her husband, Mr. Howel **Jenkins** died in 1868, and since that time she has resided with her sons. Coming to Platte City at a very early day, she lived to see nearly all the early settlers who were here at that time pass away. Having shared the vicissitudes of early life in Platte County, her history is intimately identified with it, and she was perhaps as well known as any woman who ever lived in our county. She was a member of the Episcopal Church, but her hearing having become defective of late years she was deprived of the active participation in the religious exercises to which she was so earnestly devoted.

She was essentially a Christian woman in practice as well as precept. No appeal for charity ever fell upon her unheeded, but of her means she gave freely and lavishly, while at the bedside of the sick and suffering she was ever present, a good Samaritan.

Just before her death she reminded those about her bedside that on that very evening, seven years before, her husband had paid the great debt of nature. So just when one cycle of human life had been recorded she joined the companion of her youth in the unknown world.

Appropriate funeral services were conducted by Elder **Williams** on Monday, and then this pure, noble and Christian woman was laid to rest to sleep the sleep that knows no wakening

Grange Notice:

At a regular meeting of New Market Grange No. [9?7], the Master appointed a committee to draft resolutions of respect to our lamented brother, Archibald T. **Leavel**. He was born in Madison County, Ky., on November 3d 1822, and in 1827 his parents moved to Lincoln County in the same state. In the summer of 1845 he made a public confession of his faith in Jesus Christ, and he was immersed by Elder Carroll **Kendrick** into the merits of the death of Christ, from which time till his death he continued an earnest and faithful

April 30, 1875 (Continued)

Christian. In the fall of 1852, he with his family moved to Platte County, Mo., and settled on the farm on which he died.

On Tuesday night, March 30th, he was seized with a congestive chill, and continued to grow worse until Thursday morning at 9 o'clock and ten minutes, when he fell asleep in the arms of Him in whom he had so long trusted. Oh, may we have faith, as it was manifested in our beloved brother.

We tender to his family and friends our sympathy and kindest regards; may his weeping wife and children see that another link binds them forever to heaven. But, while we mourn to give him up, may our Father prepare us to say, 'thy will be done, not ours.'

How peaceful the grave, its silence how deep. Oh, soft are the breezes that play 'round the tomb where the way worn traveler lays his body down, there to repose forever.

Resolved, That in the death of Bro. **Leavel**, New Market Grange No. [9_7], has lost one of its best members, and the community a useful citizen.

Resolved, That while we commend his virtues to all of our order, we, of New Market Grange, will cherish his memory with the fondest recollection.

Resolved, That we deeply sympathize with his family in their sad bereavement.

Resolved, that these resolutions be furnished the county papers for publication and a copy be presented to the family of the deceased.

B.F. [**Shopse**?]

G. W. **Field** Committee

Isaac **Dean**

May 7, 1875

Died:

Mr. B.F. **McNemar**, an old citizen of this county, died of pneumonia, at his residence a few miles east of Platte City, last Saturday night. He was buried at the City cemetery on Monday. Mr. **McNemar** was born in Hardy County, West Virginia, May 28, 1824, where he lived until November 1856, when he came to Missouri. He was an honest man and a good citizen. He leaves a widow and two daughters- one single and the other married to Mr. Martin **Brown** of this county.

Birth's, Death's and Marriages from the Platte City Missouri "Landmark"

Friday, May 14, 1875

Married:

Our young friend Jacob T. **Busey**, of the late grocery firm of **Busey** and **Sloan** was married Thursday evening of last week to the beautiful Miss Fannie **Murley**, of Platte City. The ceremony took place at the Baptist Church, Rev J.W. **Brown**, officiating, and was witnessed by a large number of friends who wish the handsome young couple all the happiness that wedded life vouch safes, and in this wish none more sincerely joins than THE LANDMARK.

Friday, May 21, 1875

On the night of the 14th inst, a party of unknown men rode up to the house of Ben **Ivens**, a negro, in Layfayette county, called him to the door and perfectly riddled him with buckshot, killing him instantly. The coroner's inquest threw no light on the dark transaction.

Friday, May 28, 1875

Died:

On Thursday morning, the 13th, inst. Mrs. Sally **Layton**, consort of Perry M. **Layton**, in the 23d year of her age, after a painful illness of ten days.

The deceased was beloved by all who knew her. She was truly a pattern of excellence in all the various relations she sustained in life. She was an affectionate companion, a tender mother, a kind and obliging neighbor and friend and a sincere Christian. For many years she had followed the precepts of her Saviour and was a bright example of Christian humility and devotion. She had endeared herself to a large circle of friends by her many virtues. She was a true and faithful member of the Salem congregation. She was unexpectedly taken from her family, but she had her lamp trimmed and burning. Her pure spirit has gone to join the bright hosts in the paradise of God—that blissful region where sorrow, sickness and death are unknown. [Tribute following, not recorded here]

June 4, 1875

Mrs. Granville **Adkins** was buried in the City cemetery, this place, on Tuesday afternoon last. She died in Leavenworth. Particulars, next week.

June 11, 1875

Death of Mrs. Adkins

—Last week we made brief mention of the death of Mrs. Della M. **Adkins**, wife of Mr. Granville **Adkins**, but want of time prevented a more extended notice at the time. She died in Leavenworth, Kansas, on the 31st of May, in the 39th year of her age. The disease which finally resulted in her death was dropsy of many years' duration and involving much mental and bodily suffering. Mrs. **Adkins** was the daughter of Prof. **Patterson**, for many years prominent educator in Platte City. Under his tutelage and parental care his daughter acquired an accomplished and most through education. Of fine literary tastes and superior musical skill she was, during all the shifting scenes of her chequered life, an attractive ornament to the society in which she lived. Of a religious turn of mind, she early became a member of the Episcopal Church and died in that faith. Mrs. **Adkins'** remains were brought to Platte City and interred in the private burying grounds of Mrs. **Marshall**, followed to their final resting place by many of the friends of her early years, who dropped a tear of sympathy and sorrow in her untimely grave.

Death of Miss Fannie Bronaugh--

Miss. Fannie M. **Bronaugh**, the beautiful, accomplished and amiable daughter of Mr. John **Bronaugh**, died at the residence of her father, near Barry, in Clay County on the 2d of June inst., after a very painful illness of nine weeks. She was born December 2d [?] and was consequentially less than twenty-four years old when death claimed it's fair victim. She was buried at Barry with the ceremonial [?] to the Patrons of Husbandry, of which order she was a zealous member. The solemn religious services were conducted by Rev. Mr. **Betts**, of the Episcopal Church of Kansas City. Many years ago Miss **Bronaugh** became a member of the Christian Church and lived and died a devout, ardent and exemplary communicant of that church. Blessed with a liberal education and endowed with all the accomplishments which wealth and parental devotion

June 11, 1875 (Continued)

could bestow, she exercised her graces of person and mind to make herself the pet of all who knew her of came within the place of her sweet innocence.

The universal grief and unanimous respect expressed when her death became known, enhanced in some slight degree the love all bore her, and how her memory will long be cherished as one of the highest things of earth.

True it is that Death loves a shining maid and that the loveliest die early, if death perforce, must come to one so young and so radiantly fair, it could not come in lovelier guise—all the flowers abloom with the perfume of May—all the roses redolent of June—the trees aglow with sunshine and thrilling with the bird songs of Summer—all nature regal in her garniture of buds and grasses. The farewell spoken here on earth become joyous greetings from the angel bands in Heaven. Sleep sweetly; our's the cross; thine the crown.

Died:

Near Barry, Clay County, Missouri, June 24th, Miss Fanny **Bronaugh**, daughter of Mr. John **Bronaugh**.

Few young ladies have been so loved and respected among a large circle of friends and acquaintances as Miss **Bronaugh**. To a good mind, trained in the best schools, was joined a heart filled with the noblest and most generous impulses. She was a dutiful daughter and a devoted friend. It would be scarcely be believed that one so modest and retiring could be so firm and resolute when occasion required it.

When a young lady in the full bloom of womanhood dies our hearts are filled with sorrow and regret. But when that lady is endowed with all the virtues which adorn her sex; a mind pure and unselfish; a character free from spot or blemish; a heart overflowing with the love of home, family and friends, and a deportment in which modestly and dignity mark the gentleness and sensibility of her nature—when one such dies the language of ordinary panegyric is inadequate to express our grief.

Although she has passed from this earth forever, yet the perfume of her many virtues will linger in our memories, and leave a fragrance among the dead hours of the past that will cause us to revert to them with pleasure.

Not many months since, when a babe lay in its shroud and its mother prostrated with grief, this young lady kept vigil over it through the long dreary night. Oh how little then did we think that she would so soon join our little Mary in the spirit world.

We respectfully tender our sympathy to the good old mother, the excellent father, and the devoted sister and brother.

June 18, 1875

Born:

To Elder W. H. **Williams**, on the morning of the 19th of May, a son, weighing six pounds.

Nuptials:

Married **Coleman-Oldham**

On the evening of the [10th] inst., at the residence of the bride's parents in Leavenworth city, by the Rev. [_?_] **Woodward**,. Thomas H. **Coleman** Esq., Of this place to Miss Hallie E. **Oldham**, of the former city, and formerly of this county. [NOTE: This was a very long announcement and thus not copied here in its entirety].

June 25, 1875

Married:

From the Leavenworth "Times" we see that our old friend and country man, Mr. Charles H. **Lamar**, was married to Miss Mattie **Hawn**, at the Episcopal Church, in Leavenworth last Monday. Rev. J.N. **Lee** officiating.

Died:

We learn that Mrs. John **Flannery**, nee Miss Sheba **Blanton** a young lady well known and greatly beloved by the citizens of Platte County died at the residence of her husband in Waterville, Kansas, last Saturday.

Birth's, Death's and Marriages from the Platte City Missouri "Landmark"

July 16, 1875

At Rest:

Death of Mrs. Jesse **Morin**

Again we are sadly reminded of the fact that our pioneer men and women are rapidly passing away. How many within the Last year have laid aside their burdens and crossed over to the other side, it is hard to tell; but certainly it is a startling number and gives us warning that the ancient landmarks of the Platte Purchase are soon to be obliterated forever.

Mrs. Zerelda V. **Morin**, wife of Maj. Jess **Morin**, died at the family residence in Platte City last Tuesday evening, July 13th 1875. This announcement will doubtless be a sad surprise to all throughout this section whose good fortune it was to know Mrs. **Morin**, for scarcely was her illness known outside her immediate family circle before its culmination came and death asserted its might.

Mrs. **Morin** was the daughter of John and Sarah **Hughes**, and was born in Jessamine County, Kentucky, July 31st, 1813. Her father was a well known Baptist preacher, and doubtless from his pious example he inculcated her well known religious zeal; a zeal not ostentatious or puritanical, but earnest, practible and charitable. She was married to Maj. Jess **Morin** in Howard County, Missouri, August 18th, 1831, and has lived in Platte County since May 1837, honored and beloved by all who knew her, a devoted wife, a tender mother, a kind and considerate neighbor and a most exemplary member of society. Her children she has been spared to see grow up around her honored and prosperous citizens. For many years she had been a member of the Christian church and died in its faith.

The funeral services took place Wednesday afternoon at the family residence, Rev. Jeremiah **Clay** and J.W. **Brown** officiating, after which loving hands, performed the last rites of sepulture.

To the stricken husband, who after the rugged war of life, is left to travel down the shady pathway alone, the companion of his youthful toils and inspirer of his young ambitions having gone before; to the children who must now experience the utter lack of a mothers love; to the numerous relatives and that more numerous throng of friends attached to herby her many virtues, the sympathies of all are extended.

Her memory is safe because her radiant virtues constitute her monument more imperishable than marble or bronze.

July 23, 1875

Death of Emma Johnston—

Emma **Johnston**, daughter of Mrs. Georgia **Johnston**, aged about fourteen years, died at the residence of her mother, about three miles East of Platte City, Thursday night of last week, after a long and distressing illness. She was a young lady of many accomplishments and was beloved by all for her amiable character and kind and loving disposition. She was a student at Daughters College where her activity of mind and cheerfulness of disposition made her the favorite of both faculty and classmates. Her remains were buried in the Platte City cemetery last Saturday.

July 30, 1875

Ellington Casper, who was killed by falling in a well which he was cleaning, was buried last Thursday. The Lexington Fire Company No 2, of which he was a member, followed his remains to the grave. Mr. **Casper** leaves a wife and six children in a destitute condition.

Marriages:

--On the 19th inst, by the Rev H.W. **Curran**, near Weston, Mr. Robert **Murdock** and Miss Carrie **Minter**.

--On the 27th inst., at the residence of Mr. J. C. **Davis**, by Elder W.H. **Williams**, Mr. W. W. **Davis** and Miss Melissa D. **Corbin**, all of Platte County.

We hope our friend's shadow may not grow less this hot weather.

Died:

On Friday, the 23d inst., at his home near Camden Point, in this county, after a lingering illness, of dropsy, William B. **Shanks**

July 30, 1875 (Continued)

Mr. **Shanks** was in every sense of the word one of the best citizens of Platte County. He was a member of the Christian Church, a true friend, possessed a warm and tender heart, and leaves, beside a devoted wife and children, a host of friends to mourn his early death.

--On the 26th inst., at the residence of her son, A.M.J. **Handley**, near Second Creek, Mrs. Sarah A. **Handley**, wife of James **Handley**, aged 75 years, 4 months and 5 days.

--Henry, infant son of J.H. and C.T. **Baker**, died at the residence of the parents in Platte City, on the 22d inst., aged twenty-two months and ten days.

August 6, 1875

Mary Woodson, infant daughter of Mr. And Mrs. C.P. **Armstrong**, of St. Joseph, died last Saturday morning.

DIED:

Near Farley, July 30th, 1875 of abscess of the spine, Mrs. Martha E **Cole**, wife of John R. **Cole**.

Mrs. **Cole** was born in Woodford Co. Ky., January 11th, 1835, and moved to Platte City Mo with her father, Wm **Ford**, when she was about two years old, and was married to John R. **Cole** September 28, 1853. She had lived in the vicinity in which she died since that time. She leaves a devoted husband and six children, one of which is only a week old, to mourn her loss, while she has gone to reunite with three children who have preceded her across the Jordan of Death.

Words of praise to Mrs. **Cole** would be fulsome to those who have lived in close proximity to her for the space which she had lived in this community. Warm and impulsive in her nature she was generous to a fault. No needy applicant ever passed her household with their wants uncared for, while at the same time, to her prudence and frugality, indomitable industry and perseverance, is owing in great measure the raising and educating of a large family, and securing with the assistance of her husband a comfortable homestead &c.

August 6, 1875 (Continued)

Truly is this an affliction, the greatest that could have befallen this family, but he who tempers the wind to the shorn lamb has promised to watch over her dear lambs with all a mothers care. But to the father of those children, the husband of the departed, who is more fully competent of appreciating the magnitude of the loss he has sustained, how shall we offer him consolation except it be from that inspiration which that teaches that there is a just God, and that "He doeth all things well". Mrs. **Cole** was known and appreciated in her neighborhood for her kindness. She was a member of the Christian Church for several years before her death.

May we not sincerely hope that in the great future when again we meet those parted from here in sorrow, that our joy may be equally as great as our parting is grievous now.

--On July 26th at the residence of her son, A.M.I. **Handley**, in Platte County, Mo., after a short illness, Mrs. Sarah A. **Handley**, aged 75 years, four months and fifteen days.

The deceased was born in Marion County, KY March 11, 1800, and was married to James **Handley**, October 16, 1816. She moved to Missouri in March 1867. Seven children preceded her to the grave. She leaves three sons in Missouri and three daughters in Kentucky to mourn her loss. She professed religion and joined the Methodist Church South in 1868 and lived a pious and devoted Christian life, bearing and suffering for the Saviours sake in patience and humility, the ills of life and died in peace with the full assurance of "entering into that rest that remaineth to the people of God," and left an example in life worthy of [___?___] and recommending her religion o her bereaved sons and daughters. May they follow her example with the full assurance of meeting a kind and affectionate mother in a better land. She was kind, faithful, and true as a wife and mother

August 13, 1875

Nuptials:

On the 8th inst., at the **Brady** house, in this City by Esquire **Hatton**, Mr. Timothy **Phillips** to Miss Emma S. **Ducoing**,, both of Leavenworth, Kansas.

On the 3d inst., at the residence of the officiating minister, by the Rev Thomas **Hurst,** Mr. William C. **Spencer** to Miss Mary E. **Figley**, all of Platte County.

August 13, 1875 (Continued)

At the residence of the bride's parents on Sunday August 1, by Rev. Mr. **Burruss**, Mr. Virgil **Wood** to Miss Fannie **Searcy**, daughter of Mr. Nat **Searcy**, all of Platte. [This entry shortened]

August 20, 1875

Married—On the 15th inst., in Lawrence, Kansas, at the residence of the bride's father, by the Rev. Mr. **Caruthers**, Mr. H. S. **Kline**, of the *Advocate* of this City, to Miss. Mary D. **Reed**, of the former city.

We bespeak for the happy couple a long life of prosperity and conjugal bliss.

A Strange Wedding--On the 10th inst., Elder B. **Waller**, at Smithville, in Clay County, solemnized the nuptials of Mr. James **Jesse** and Miss **Grinestead**, both of Platte County. Mr. **Jesse** is terribly deformed. His arms are without joints and his hands and feet are what are called "club". His legs are badly deformed and his manner of locomotion is to straddle a low chair, and by moving his short legs manages to get about tolerably well. The bride is entirely dumb and nearly deaf, the result of an attack of scarlet fever many years ago. THE LANDMARK extends its congratulations to the happy pair.

Arsenic and Pistol—

Dr. A. J. **Larey** Commits Suicide:

One of the most terrible and startling events that have occurred in Platte county for many years, took place at the village of Iatan, about thirteen miles northwest of Platte City on the evening of the 16th inst. The air has been full of rumors concerning the terrible affair, some of the wildly at variance with the facts; others circumstantially correct. We have taken the trouble to investigate the affair and are enabled to detail the circumstances with accuracy. We depend for our information upon a letter received by us from Mr. R.R. **Rose** and a letter received by Sheriff **Coffey** from Mr. William **Calvert**, both gentlemen being well acquainted with the facts.

Birth's, Death's and Marriages from the Platte City Missouri "Landmark"

August 20, 1875 (Continued)

Mr. **Rose** informs us that on the afternoon of last Monday, as Dr. **Larey** was leaving his dwelling house, he informed his wife that if he did anything desperate while he was gone she must not be alarmed but must forgive him. Not knowing his desperate intentions she paid no particular attention to his language.

It appears that he then went across the street to his office and took a large quantity of arsenic and then went into the ante room adjoining. He soon returned and found Mr. **Bailey** and Mr. James **Gittinger** in the office and told them what he had done. He spoke to them about his business and told **Bailey** to take his library, read his books and take care of them. He then went and got his day book and handed it to Mr. **Gittinger** and requested him to give some credits to parties who had paid him money the day before. He then started for the ante room, and as he entered the door he pulled it half shut, holding it with his right hand; he then took out his pocket pistol and placing the muzzle just above the left ear, looking Mr. **Bailey** straight in the eyes, fired the fatal shot and fell to the floor. It was about four o'clock when he committed the deed, and his death occurred at 7:30 P.M.

Such, in brief are the facts of this most distressing affair. The cause is enveloped in mystery. We, however see that it has been telegraphed abroad that the Dr. had for several days been drinking to excess and that upon recovering from his spree learned that several of his patients had required his professional services in the meantime, and that one of them, a warm personal friend, had died. We give the rumor for what it is worth. Certain it is, though, that Dr. **Larey** was devoted to his profession and particularly sensitive about his professional honor. Remorse for apparent [?] to his duties may have caused him to commit the rash deed.

Dr. **Larey**, we believe was a South Carolinian, and came to Kansas during the troubles in 1856, residing for several years in Atchison county. Removing to Iatan in this county, he at once entered upon a large and lucrative practice, which he retained until his death. He married Miss **Hudson** several years ago, and his domestic relations have been of the most pleasant character. He leaves a most interesting family. Dr. **Larey** was an accomplished physician and surgeon, a man of wealth and influence and warm hearted and generous to a fault. Few men had more friends or will be more generally lamented. His tragic death has cast a gloom wherever he was known, and it will be many a day before his place will be supplied. "After life's fitful fever he sleeps well."

August 20, 1875 (Continued)

A Pioneer Dead:

Death of James **Fox**, one of the very Oldest Citizens of Platte County

James **Fox** died at his residence, four miles south of Platte City, last Saturday, Aug. 14th. The death of such a man deserves more than a passing notice, for the history of his life is a history of Platte County and the Platte purchase.

The subject of this notice was born in Farquier County, Virginia, November 11th, 1790. He was raised and lived in Virginia until 1836, when imbibing the spirit of adventure, he joined the vast tide of emigration that was wetting in toward the great west, he removed to Howard county Missouri with his wife Miss Lucinda **Eskridge**. He remained in Howard county only one year. Attracted by the wonderful stories of the fertility of the then noted Platte purchase, he came to Platte county and settled upon and preempted the farm (October 15, 1837) upon which he lived the remainder of his life. His only child, Mr. William A **Fox**, one of our oldest and best citizens and his aged wife alone survive him, the latter a hopeless invalid. Mr. **Fox** literally died of old age, having been confined to his room since last December. Although a pious, God-fearing man, he only publicly made a profession of religion about one year ago when he joined the Methodist Episcopal Church, South. His remains were buried at the family burying ground upon the farm where he had lived and died.

Such, in brief is an epitome of the history of James **Fox**, famiarly known as "Uncle Jimmy", a [?] that history must remain incomplete, for it is beyond our power to record the thrilling events that made up his romantic career. He came to Platte county when it was home of the Indians and was a wilderness. He lived to see it grow from its [?] pioneer population to its present populas condition-the very finest agricultural county in Missouri.

Mr. **Fox** was emphatically a hard worker, and it is said that he performed more hard physical labor than any other man in the county. He was restless and discontented unless he was actively engaged in his farm duties. He was essentially honest and during all his long life he never was engaged directly or indirectly in a law-suit. He was a kind neighbor and a great citizen, respected by all who knew him...

Birth's, Death's and Marriages from the Platte City Missouri "Landmark"

August 27, 1875

Married:

On the evening of the 25th inst., at her brother's residence in this city, by the Rev Mr. **Ellis**, Mr. J.R. **Luty**, of Bismark, Kansas to Miss Bell **Edwards** of this place. We wish the happy couple a long life of happiness and prosperity.

Died:

Of typhoid Dysentery on the 26th of July, 1857, at the residence of her son, A.M.I. **Handley**, near Barry, Platte county, Missouri, Mrs. Sarah A. **Handley**, wife of James **Handley** in the 75th year of her age.

The subject of this sketch was born in Marion County, Ky., on the 11th of March, 1800. On the 18th of October 1816 she was married to her now deeply afflicted husband, who still survives her and is now in his eighty-second year, with whom she lived for fifty-nine years in the most happy marital relations. She was the mother of twelve children, seven of whom have preceded her to the shores of that undiscovered country lying beyond the darkling waters of the stream of death. Five children still survive her, three sons who sat by her bedside to comfort her in her sickness, and painfully witness her final conflict with the king of terrors and two absent daughters who mourn their irreparable loss. She was a pious sweet tempered Christian, having united with the Methodist Episcopal Church South at Milestown, Ky in October 1853, in whose communion she remained a consistent and exemplary member to the close of life, giving to her friends satisfactory evidence of her peaceful departure and glorified rest beyond the grave. In March 1857, she removed with her husband and family from Kentucky to Missouri and settled in Platte County, where she lived until the close of her long and useful life. As a helpful, conciliating and affectionate mother, and a sweet tempered and obliging neighbor, she will be greatly missed. And, Oh! What must be the intensity of the grief which wings his soul who feels the cords loosening which have for 59 years bound him to her who was the object of his youthful love, the companion of his mature years and the comfort of his old age. How memory will revel in the past, and linger about and dote on the years of long ago. But the separation will be short. The feeble steps of age have almost brought him to the margin of the water, which separates his county from here. –O.L. **Allen**

At the residence of the parents,

Three miles south of Platte City, on the 19th inst. Eddie Oscar **Cooper**, age one year, son of John and Martha **Cooper**.

August 27, 1875 (Continued)

Death of Cornelius Cooper—

Mr. Cornelius **Cooper**, one of the oldest citizens of Platte County, died at his residence three miles west of Platte City, on the 18th inst. Mr. **Cooper** was born in Franklin County Virginia June 22nd, 1802. He spent his young manhood in his ancestral home, and there married Miss. **Harkrider**. He afterwards removed to Indiana and in 1844 came to Platte County, Missouri and settled upon the farm upon which he resided till his death. Mr. **Cooper** belonged to no church, but was strictly a Christian man. His honesty and integrity was proverbial, and no man ever sustained a higher character as a neighbor and citizen. Five children survive him to honor his name and commerate his virtues.

September 10, 1875

Married:

At the residence of the bride's father August 31st 1875 by the Rev. Mr. **Newman**, Mr. J.F. **Justus** to Miss Mildred **Blesdoe**, all of Lafayette County.

Died:

At the residence of his parents six miles East of Platte City on the 28th day of August, Richard H. **Jesse**, aged one year and six days, son of John and Adaline **Jesse**. [Tribute not copied]

Death of Another Aged Resident of Platte County

Mrs. Catherine **Coffey**, relict of the late Rev. Dr. R.N. **Coffey** and mother of our worthy sheriff Fr. E.McD **Coffey** died at the residence of the daughter Mrs. Mary **Bradley**, near Camden Point in this county, last Sunday morning, the 5th inst. This announcement will doubtless be a sad surprise to the many friends of the family throughout this state and Kentucky, for during her long and useful life she endeared herself to all with whom she came in contact.

September 10, 1875 (Continued)

Mrs. **Coffey** was the daughter of Joseph **McCormack**, of Lincoln county, Kentucky, the progenitor of one of the oldest and best families in Kentucky, and was born Aug. 9th 1799. She was reared and educated in the county of her birth and in May 1818 was married to Dr. R.N. **Coffey**. For many years they lived in Madison County, Kentucky, and finally removed to Platte County, Missouri, locating at Camden Point, where her venerable husband died in 1867, after a ministry of twenty-five years in the Baptist Church. At the bedside of the dying women were her three living children, and she expressed herself then as being fully reconciled to die. The funeral services were conducted by Eld W.H. **Thomas**, at the Baptist church near Camden Point, on Monday last, when her remains were consigned to mother earth by the tender hands of her old friends and neighbors.

In every relation of life Mrs. **Coffey** was a most excellent women. She was educated, practical, generous, considerate and tender hearted, and leaves the world regretted by all.

George Martin

Who committed suicide by shooting himself with a rifle, near Mt. Florence, Kans., on the 26th of July, was a former resident of Platte county and lived near Camden point. He was a brother in law of Mr. Joshua **Pumphrey**. He was an excellent citizen and a man of some wealth and prominence; but the grasshoppers destroyed his crops and he became so much depressed mentally, that in a fit of insanity he terminated his existence.

We Regret to Learn:

That Ernest L., son of Mr. John B. **Flannery** and lady, died at the residence of the parents, in Kansas 'City on the 5th inst., aged eighteen months. The remains were brought to Platte City and interred in the City Cemetery on Tuesday. The child was a bright, active little fellow. The pride and joy of its parents and their grief at their bereavement is intense. They have the sympathy of their many friends in Platte.

Birth's, Death's and Marriages from the Platte City Missouri "Landmark"

September 24, 1875

Killed by a horse—

On last Sunday evening a man named **Olds**, living at Mr. Elliott J. **Miller's**, four miles north of Platte city, sustained fatal injuries under the following circumstances: **Olds** was riding a horse belonging to Mr. **Miller** which was rather wild and untractable. When crossing the railroad track near Mr. **Miller's** residence the horse suddenly reared up and fell down the embankment. Mr. **Olds** was caught underneath the horse and both laid motionless until Mr. **Miller**, who witnessed the accident, and Mr. W.E. **Stitt** went to the rescue. The injured man was removed to the house but never recovered his consciousness, and died on Monday evening. His injuries were chiefly of the chest and internal. He was a man about fifty years old, quiet, sober, intelligent and gentlemanly.

Died—

Mrs. Cornelia **Chinn**, wife of Mr. A.N. **Chinn**, living three miles east of Platte City, died last Friday evening and was buried on Sunday at Platte City, Elder **Williams** preaching the funeral discourse. Mrs. **Chinn** was the daughter of Mrs. Julia **Pullins** and was about twenty-five years old and had been married about six years. She leaves three children, the youngest an infant only a few days old. Mrs. **Chinn** was a member of the Christian Church and in every respect a most estimable woman, beloved by all who knew her.

October 1, 1875

Miss Lizzie Belt, daughter of Hon. Geo W. **Belt** was married to George D. **Green** Esq. A prominent young attorney at St. Joseph last Wed., Particulars next week.

The wife of Mr. Wm Tatman died last Friday. We have not yet learned any of the particulars. She was however one of the oldest citizens of the county and a most estimable lady.

October 8, 1875

An old Landmark Gone

Henry **DeBard**, one of the oldest citizens of Platte County, departed this life on Wednesday last at about four o'clock P.M. He was born in Clark county, Kentucky, November 24, 1801, and removed to Mount Sterling, in the same State, in 1822, where he resided until 1841, when he removed to Platte City, Mo, where he has ever since lived, being a resident of this county for thirty-five years.

He was, perhaps the oldest tyler in the United States, and beyond a doubt in the State of Missouri.

He is gone, and has left a record for faithfulness, integrity, and sobriety that challenges the universal approbastion of those by whom he was surrounded. May he rest in peace.

His remains were interred with Masonic honors on Thursday last.

We will have more to say of his history in the future.

October 15, 1875

An Old Fashioned German Wedding—

A notable wedding occurred near Farley in Lee Township, in this county, on Thursday of last week. It was a regular old fashioned German wedding, celebrated after the customs of the Fatherland. The contracting parties were Mr. August **Schmuttie**, of Farley, and Miss Lou **Meyer**, of Lee Township. The ceremony was performed by Rev. Mr. **Johnston**, of the German Lutheran Church, at the church, and was witnessed by a large number of friends and acquaintances. After the ceremony was performed the bridal party repaired to the residence of the bride's father, Mr. Randolph **Meyer**, one of the leading citizens of the section, and from that time until the next morning the joyous festivities were kept up, almost the entire community participating. To give an idea of the extent of the preparations for the entertainment of the guests we will merely say that an entire beef was cooked, also five dozen chickens and that the beverages consisted of ten kegs of beer, with wine and liquors in due proportion. In the interval of feasting, dancing and various other amusements were indulged in, and a more pleasant occasion has seldom been observed in this county. All the parties are of the highest respectability and are among our wealthiest and most prosperous German citizens. To the happy bride and groom THE LANDMARK extends its congratulations and its wishes for their long lives and perfect happiness and prosperity.

Birth's, Death's and Marriages from the Platte City Missouri "Landmark"

October 15, 1875 (Continued)

Death of an Estimable Lady—

Mrs. **Oleschlager**, wife of Mr. F. H. **Oleschlager**, died of puerperal fever, at the residence of her husband near Farley, in this County, on Wednesday, October 6th. Mrs. **Oleschlager** was a highly cultivated and refined lady and was universally beloved. Her untimely death has cast a gloom over the entire neighborhood, where she was known and admired for her generosity, amiability and nobility of character.

October 22, 1875

Married— The 14th inst., at the residence of L.A. **Hurst** by Rev Thos. **Hurst**, Mr. Wm **Figley** to Miss Letty D. **Byons**, all of Platte County, Mo

Married—At the residence of Capt Wm **Chestnut**, five miles east of Platte City, by Elder W. H **Williams**, on the 19th inst., Mr. G. F. **Clemmings** of Platte City to Mrs. Kate **Callahan**. [Continued, not readable]

Married— At the residence of the bride's parents, near Smithville, on the 14th inst, by Rev R.B. **Waller**, Mr. John W. **Spratt** of Smithville to Miss [?] **Thatcher**, daughter of Mr. Daniel **Thatcher** of Platte City.

Attendants—Mr. John **Wood** and Miss Bettie **Berryman**, and Mr. [Jefferson] **Vance** and Miss Dolly **Searce**.

Mr. **Spratt** is the leading merchant of Smithville, and one of the most through gentlemen in America. His bride is beautiful, amiable, and intelligent; so congratulations are due both parties, and THE LANDMARK extends its best wishes and hopes for their long lives and perfect happiness.

October 22, 1875 (Continued)

Obituary

Mrs. A.T. **Holt** died in Farley, Friday October 15th. A noble women is gone, truly it is said that our brightest and most valued gems are taken away by the Divine being. Cut down in the first flush of matured womanhood by the relentless hand of Death, she leaves and aching void in the hearts of her many friends which can never be filled. A member of the Christian Church, her's has ever been the life of a Christian, loved by all with whom she came in contact; sincerely do we deplore her early death. [Tribute not copied]

Death—Mr. E.C. **Powell** died at his residence in Farley, in this County, on the 16th inst., after a protracted illness, aged about sixty-five years. Mr. **Powell** was a prominent and influential citizen and few [_____] than he did the confidence of those with whom he associated. He at various times occupied positions of trust and importance, and always discharged their duties honestly and ably. Few better men that Esquire **Powell** have lived or died in Platte County.

October 29, 1875

An Elegant Wedding—A Select number of intimate friends and relatives assembled at the residence of Hon. Thomas **Quinn**, four miles north of Platte City, on Wednesday, Oct 27th, to witness the nuptials of Maj. Geo T. **Jones** and Miss Delia **Marshall**. The ceremony was performed by Elder F.W. **Allen** and was beautiful and impressive. Earnest congratulations followed, after which the company sat down to a wedding feast, where the tables fairly groaned beneath their weight of good things, and such a warm and lavish hospitality as Mr. and Mrs. **Quinn** alone can dispense added zest to an already happy occasion. Few occasions have occurred in Platte County where there was more real enjoyment among the guests and more genuine happiness manifest in those more intimately concerned. For it was a true love match, and the aurcole of supreme happiness that bends above such a union never shone with a brighter and holier light. Both of them young and gifted, and bound about with friends as true and steadfast as books of steel, the future opens up a joyous vista. It is THE LANDMARK's sincerest wish that all their subsequent journey through life may prove a realization of their present hopes and a fulfillment of all friends' most happy prophecies.

Birth's, Death's and Marriages from the Platte City Missouri "Landmark"

October 29, 1875 (Continued)

The attendants of the happy couple were Mr. George **Mason**, of Platte City, and Miss Hattie **Hamlin** of Leavenworth, and Mr. T.L. **Thomas** of Platte City and Miss Florence **Miller**, of Leavenworth. Among the guests present were Mrs. F.G. **Gaylord**, C.B. **Hawley** and lady, C.T. **Murdock** and lady, Robt. **Hardesty** and lady, Ben. **Perry** and lady, Miss Janie **Clemings**, Miss Hattie **Collins**, Jo **Parrott** and lady, Messrs Ben W. **Gilbert**, C.M. **Cartwright**, W.W. **Rixey**, W.T. **Jenkins** and many others.

Married—The ceremony that united the lives and fortunes of Mr. Julius **Becker** of Weston, and Miss Emma **Magers**, of Platte City, was preformed by Rev. P. **Ziswyler**, at the residence of the bride's father, Mr. Frederick **Magers**, in Platte City, on the 21st inst. A large number of friends witnessed the nuptial ceremony and participated in the wedding festivities. For a very liberal remembrance of this office in the way of table delicacies, THE LANDMARK desires to return its thanks, and also to extend its best wishes for a happy and prosperous career for the joyous young pair.

--On the 26th of Oct., 1875, Mr. James C. **Wilkerson**, Esq., to Miss Amanda V. **Logan**, at the residence of James **Miller**, by Rev. D.F. **Bone**, all of Platte County Missouri:

> Together may they sweetly live
>
> Together may they die
>
> Each a starry crown receive
>
> And reign above the sky

--At Hampton, Oct. 22nd, at the residence of the bride's father, by M.A. **Flynn**, Esq., Mr. James **Algier** of South Cedar Falls, Kansas, to Miss Alice **Malott** of Hampton.

--Mr. James **Morris**, and old and highly respected citizen of Green Township, died at his residence near Camden Point, last Monday, aged about sixty five years.

Resolutions: Adopted by the Sunday School House near Ridgely, upon the death of Rev. John P. **Keen**

Whereas, It has pleased our Heavenly Father in his mysterious providence, to remove from our midst and from the field of usefulness, the faithful and efficient superintendent of our Sabbath School, Rev. John P. **King**, therefore,

Birth's, Death's and Marriages from the Platte City Missouri "Landmark"

October 29, 1875 (Continued)

Resolved, That we regard the death of Bro. **Keen** as a calamity, not only to our Sunday school but to the church and community at large. He was a devoted Christian, a faithful friend, a good neighbor, and an honest man. In all the relations of life, whether as a minister, Sunday school Superintendent or private citizen, he was an earnest and zealous worker in the cause of Christ.

Resolved, That while we lament this sad affliction to us as a Sabbath School and as a community, we believe that our loss is his infinite gain. His devoted life and uniform Christian character leave no doubt in our minds of his acceptance with God, and we bow with humble resignation to the behest of Him who is too wise to err and too good to do wrong.

Resolved, that we deeply sympathize with his afflicted children in their sad bereavement, and we can but commend them, with prayerful, sympathizing hearts, to Him who has promised to be a father to the fatherless. May His merciful providence supervise their discipline and instruction, and may those who have them in charge bring them up in the nurture and admonition of the Lord.

Resolved, That a copy of these resolutions be sent to the family of the deceased, and a copy be sent to the county papers for publication.

Obituary—At a meeting of the officers and members of Farley Lodge, No 177, I.O.O.F. held in their Hall on the evening of Oct 16th, 1875; the following preamble and resolutions were unanimously adopted:

Whereas, Mrs. **Oelschlager**, the wife of our much esteemed brother, Frederic H. **Oelschlager**, has been by the mysterious hand of death, removed from the embrace of an affectionate family, as well as from a large circle of friends who are mourning their loss in sadness.

Resolved, Therefore, that this lodge extend to brother **Oelschlager** and family, that heartfelt sympathy and fraternal condolence, which are attributes of every true Odd Fellow, and that we do all that can be done to assuage the sorrow, and remove the gloom which has so recently eclipsed the brightest hope of a once happy family.

Resolved, That in this dispensation of providence, we are taught the time honored lesson that "in the midst of life we are in death" We therefore bow in humble submission to the will of Him who supremely holds a governing power over all the earth.

Resolved, That a copy of these resolutions be presented Brother **Oelschlager**, and that another copy be forwarded to THE LANDMARK with a request for publication.

- C.L. **Banning**
- J.W. **McMichael**   Committee
- L.T. **Oliver**

November 5, 1875

Ben Gilbert Joins the Benedicts

There was a quiet little wedding at the residence of Hon. Clay **Park**, In Atchison, Kansas, last Tuesday morning. The high contracting parties were Mr. Ben W. **Gilbert**, deputy County Clerk of Platte County, Missouri, and Miss Belle **Armstrong**, daughter of Hon. C. P. **Armstrong**, of New Market. The officiating minister was Rev. J. B. **Hardwicke**, of the Baptist Church of Atchison, Kansas. It was a quiet, unpretentious occasion, but none the less pleasant to all who were present; besides it was no surprise. Ben never could keep a secret, consequently he confidentially told about two hundred friends all about it before hand and has been receiving congratulations ever since. A few friends accompanied him from Platte city, and at Weston he was joined by others and at Atchison by still more; and they stood by him till the last. The ceremonial part of the affair was brief, and then came the congratulations as warm and earnest as ever sprang from hearts or fell from lips. There was a quiet, joyful little breakfast party, and then the happy pair immediately left for Wichita, Kansas, where a similar matrimonial event is said to have been on the taps and booked for yesterday.

We sharpened our pencil time and again to write this notice; but somehow we don't know how to begin or how to end. Words of ordinary compliment are not to be indulged in toward Ben and Ben's. A Platte county boy born and reared, known and beloved of nearly every man, woman and child whose acquaintance or whose friendship is worth the having: for many years the clerk the Probate Court, and for the last five years chief clerk in the County Clerk's office; educated, talented, warm-hearted, generous, magnanimous, accommodating, self-sacrificing—such is Ben **Gilbert**. So when we come to congratulate him, for all must be congratulated twice in their lives, when they marry and when they die, we find the ordinary language of congratulation and compliment unsatisfactory to ourselves and utterly inadequate. We have culled pretty bits of poetry and written soft sounding paragraphs of sentiment, only to tear them up again and condense all our hearts feel in saying, "Ben, old fellow, here's to you." The bride is one of Platte County's most beautiful, amiable, and intelligent daughters—known far and wide for her splendid social qualities.

Ben and Belle will come back in a few days, and quietly settle down in our midst as old married folks. He has scattered his wild oats, and she will cease her cruel work of breaking hearts. May the current affair of their blended lives flow on in tranquil bliss till this Mayday of life and love shall have given way to the calm that comes when there are "silver threads among the gold" and life with its fiercer passions has reached its ebb, and then, looking back over a well spent life fragrant with happy memories and joyful fruits, await together that peace that finally comes to us all.

November 12, 1875

Married—At the residence of Capt. Geo. S. **Story**, near Wichita, Kansas by Rev. Mr. **Harvey**, on Wednesday, Nov 3d, 1875, Mr. Thompson A. **Gilbert**, agent of the Kansas City, St. Joseph & Council Bluffs Railroad, at Weston, and Miss Ella **Story**.

To say that we congratulate our young friends upon this happy consummation of their hopes and loves, would be but a feeble expression of our feelings. Both of them children of Platte County, they are doubly endeared to hundreds of friends in the county of their nativity, and the warmest wishes of their hearts accompany them in their new relation. THE LANDMARK unites in this universal hope and vouchsafes for them a joyful and prosperous future.

--By Rev. Father **Beatus**, at the Catholic Church in Weston, on the 8th, inst., Mr. Edward **Brill** and Miss Dora **Noll**, all of Weston.

Attendants: Mr. Charles B. **Kurtz** and Miss Lou **Dietz**, and Mr. Jacob S. **Hamm** and Miss Gracie **Kurtz**.

A large number of friends witnessed the nuptial ceremonies, and congratulated the newly wedded pair. The contracting parties are among the best known and most popular young people of Weston, and their parents are among the oldest and best citizens of Platte County, immediately after the wedding the parties left for St. Joseph.

Married—At the residence of the bride's parents, in Clay county, on the 10th inst, by Elder P.J. **Burruss**, Mr. E.R. **Long** of Quincey, Ill., formerly of the Leland Hotel, Kansas City, to Miss Mattie **Lee**, daughter of Mr. Stephen **Lee**, of Clay county, Mo.

November 19, 1875

Matrimonial

Settle Station, Nov. 12th, 1875. On Wednesday evening, Nov 11th at the residence of Mr. Thomas **Harrington**, the bride's father, Mr. Jesse B. **Settle** and Miss Bettie **Harrington** were united in the bonds of matrimony. Rev. W.H. **Thomas**, of Pleasant Grove Baptist Church, performed the ceremony. The relatives of the bride and groom, and a few intimate friends witnessed the ceremony. Mr. C. H. **Settle** and Miss Mary **Miller** were the attendants. After the ceremony and the usual congratulations the party partook of the wedding supper which did honor to the occasion.

November 19, 1875 (Continued)

On Thursday evening, Nov. 12th, at the residence of Mr. Anderson **Miller**, the bride's father, Mr. C.H. **Settle** and Miss Mary **Miller** were joined together in the bonds of wedlock, Rev. W. H. **Thomas**, officiating minister. The two brides are cousins; the grooms, brothers. As the parties roving days are past" and they are all *settled*, we leave them, believing that ultimately more *settlers* will arrive.

November 26, 1875

Drowned—We learn from Mr. Jesse **Miller** that a young Negro man, whose name he did not learn, but who was in the employ of Mr. **Babcock**, in the lower part of the county, was drowned in Miller's Lake, on Tuesday last. The Negro had killed a duck on the lake and in a frail boat was attempting to secure it when the boat upset and the Negro was drowned. His body was recovered the same day, but no inquest was held.

Death of Judge Richard R. Rees—

Judge Richard R.**Rees**, better known throughout Western Missouri as "Uncle Dick", died at Leavenworth, Kans., last Friday morning. The event was not unexpected, for the reason that Judge **Rees** had been very sick for many weeks; and the most hopeful of his friends scarcely hoped for a favorable result. It is scarcely necessary for us to recount the life and public services of Judge **Rees**, for he is known to almost every man, women and child in the Missouri Valley. At one time he was a citizen of this county, then of Jackson County, and was also one of the original incorporators of the city of Leavenworth. For the last eight years he has been Judge of the Probate Court, and for many years previously a Justice of the Peace. Although a democrat in politics, so great was his popularity in Leavenworth he never failed of an election, political friends and enemies alike rallying to his support.

But it was not in political life that he achieved his greatest honors or won for himself the most undying fame. He was virtually the father of Masonry in the Missouri Valley, and as such his memory will be revered throughout the land. As a Mason, he was signally honored with all the positions of trust and distinction in the Order, and the same may be said of the Fraternity of Odd Fellows.

Birth's, Death's and Marriages from the Platte City Missouri "Landmark"

November 26, 1875 (Continued)

A large number of Masons and Knights Templar of Missouri attended his funeral last Sunday. Of these two eminent orders it was the largest funeral procession we ever saw. From all parts of the surrounding country the members of the orders assembled to do honor to the occasion. Leavenworth Commandery of Knights Templars, and the Lodges of Masons and Odd-Fellows, Belt Commandery, of Platte City, mounted, the Grand Lodge of Kansas, and members of the fraternity from Lawrence, Topeka, Atchison, and all the surrounding country, assembled to do honor to the mortal remains of one who had risen to distinguished eminence in the order. It was an occasion long to be remembered, and one the solemnity of which will impress itself upon the hearts and minds of thousand of friends.

No more brave and gallant heart has ceased to pulsate and respond to the appeals of benevolence and charity than Dick **Rees's**, and to his memory we proffer the underlying emblem of sacred rememberance, and a heartfelt "Peace to his ashes".

Matrimonial—

At Kansas City, by Elder P.K. **Dibble,** on the 20th inst., Mr. George A. **Warner** and Miss Arlie **Basye**, daughter of Mr. Henry **Basye**, all of Weston.

Although this announcement is a great surprise to the community at large, yet our congratulations to "Ash" and his fair bride are none the less hearty. We trust that every blessing of heaven may be showered upon the heads of our young friends and that their lives may be full of joy and prosperity.

December 17, 1875

Matrimonial—

A Very pleasant event occurred at the residence of Mr. James **Christy**, last Wednesday, Dec. 15th, It was the wedding of Mr. Henry C. **Mann** and Miss Luanna **Christy**, daughter of Mr. James **Christy**, all of this county. The interesting ceremony was performed by Eld. W.H. **Williams** in his usual graceful style, after which the assembled guests partook of the wedding feast. The happy couple immediately left for their future home near Smithville. Mr. **Mann** is a prosperous young farmer and stock trader, a through gentleman and highly respected citizen. The bride is [one] of the best known and most admired of all our Platte county ladies, beautiful, cultivated, amiable, loveable and beloved. We wish the joyous pair much happiness and prosperity and extend our thanks for their kind remembrance of THE LANDMARK.

December 17, 1875 (Continued)

--At the residence of Mr. Jas. **Prather**, in Clay county, Mo., Dec 8th, by Elder J.Z. **Taylor**, Mr. C.W. **Broadhurst** of Platte county, Mo., to Miss A.B. **Prather** of Clay county.

Died—

Miss Martha (Patsey) **Walker**, daughter of the late Dr. **Walker**, died at the residence of her mother, six miles Southeast of Platte City, on Wednesday of last week after a very brief illness. She was about seventeen years of age and was a great favorite among all who knew her. He funeral was preached at Platte City on Friday, by Rev. Mr. **Worth** of the Episcopal Church, after which her remains were brought to their last resting place beside those of her lamented father in our City Cemetery.

Mr. Ryland **Russell**, a prominent citizen of Marshall Township, died last Friday, after a brief illness of pneumonia. He was about thirty-five years old, and was highly esteemed by all who knew him.

Mr. Lewis **Shouse**, one of the oldest residents of Platte county, died at his residence, about four miles north of Weston, last Monday night, of pneumonia. He was an honest man, a good citizen and a Christian gentleman.

Mr. Perry **Walker** died at his residence in Platte City last Friday, of typhoid fever.

December 24, 1875

Sudden death—

Mrs. Ross **Price**, wife of Col Jas. A. **Price** and sister of Hon Tho F. **Price**, died suddenly of heart disease at her residence in Weston, Thursday afternoon of last week. She had been doing some shopping and making some calls and had just returned home when she complained of a smothering sensation, and suddenly fell back and expired. Mrs. **Price** was a most estimable lady in every sense of the word, and her untimely death has cast a gloom over a large circle of relatives and friends.

Birth's, Death's and Marriages from the Platte City Missouri "Landmark"

December 31, 1875

Matrimonial—

At the residence of the bride's mother, by Rev D.F. **Bone**, Mr. Robert E. **Cain** to Miss Luella **Alexander**, all of Platte County, Mo.

At Wallace, Buchanan county, on the 23d inst., by Esquire **Bryant**, Mr. Jesse **Blakely**, of Platte county, to Miss Dink **Cober**, of Buchanan county.

At the same time and by the same, John C. **Blakely** to Miss Bettie **Buford**, daughter of Col. **Buford**, all of Platte county.

The reception took place at the hospitable mansion of Mr. Felix **Blakley**, where the entire neighborhood congregated and spent a most delightful evening.

A Young woman takes her own life—

On Tuesday of last week a startling tragedy occurred at the residence of Mr. James **Burt**, living about two miles from East Leavenworth, in this county, the circumstances of which, as nearly as we can glean them, are as follows: Mr. James **Burt**, a widower and nephew of Capt. John **Burt**, had living upon his premises a family by the name of **Uttinger**, which consisted in part of several daughters, one of whom was named Missouri. This girl, aged about nineteen, is described as being very prepossessing in appearance. It is alleged that quite an intimacy sprung up between Mr. **Burt** and this girl, who part of the time was engaged as a domestic in his family. Whether or not this intimacy was of a criminal character has not developed. Certain it is, however, that the girl conceived a strong passion for Mr. **Burt**, and it was a common rumor in the neighborhood that they were engaged to be married.

Recently it came to the ears of Missouri that Mr. **Burt** was soon to be married to a lady in Atchison. Then it was that the trouble began. It is reported that recently while Mr. **Burt** was standing at a looking glass combing his hair that Miss **Uttinger** approached him from behind with a razor; but he saw her actions reflected in the mirror in time to take the razor from her, the inference being that she designed taking his life. This was a few days before the occurrence of the tragedy we are about to relate. On Thursday last the girl went to her relative, Mr. W.H.H. **Baker**, and asked for a pistol, stating that her father wanted it to shoot a hog, his rifle having a ball fast in it and being for that reason unserviceable. The pistol could not be found, whereupon she went to Mr. Dan **Borden's**, another neighbor, where she was more successful. Taking the pistol when went to Mr. **Burt's**. There were in the house, beside Mr. **Burt**, Mr. **Uttinger**, the girls father, another Mr. **Burt** and a Negro who was cutting Mr. James **Burt's** hair. Miss **Uttinger** passed through the room into the kitchen. Soon afterwards Mr. **Burt** entered the kitchen, when

December 31, 1875 (Continued)

the girl as he states, said she wanted to talk with him. He replied that he would talk to her after awhile and then left the room. Almost immediately a pistol shot was heard, and upon the party rushing to the kitchen found Miss **Uttinger** sitting upon the cook stove in a dying condition. She had placed the muzzle of the pistol against her temple and fired the fatal shot. Her brains were scattered over the room and the floor was covered with blood, presenting a horrible appearance. Esquire **Banning** was notified and as soon as possible impaneled a jury and held an inquest, developing substantially the facts as related.

There is considerable excitement in the neighborhood on account of the tragic affair. Among other rumors is one to the effect that the girl was enciente, and that her unhappy condition drove her to commit the desperate deed.

January 7, 1876

Matrimonial—

At the residence of the bride's father, B.W. **Estes**, Esq. Three and a half miles east of Platte City, by the Rev. D.F. **Bone**, on the 5th inst, Mr. Joseph P. **Lutes** to Miss Alice **Estes**; all of Platte county, Mo.

There was a large number of the friends of Mr. **Lutes** and Miss **Estes** present to witness the nuptial ceremonies and to partake of the many good things prepared as a nuptial feast. We sincerely pray them a long, happy and prosperous life, and a blessed immortality after death. D.F. **Bone**.

January 14, 1876

Matrimonial—

At the residence of the bride's parents in Atchison, Kansas by Rev J.B. **Hardwicke**, on Monday evening, January 10th 1876, Mr. Charles B. **Singleton**, formerly of Platte County to Miss Mollie F. **Price**, daughter of Hon John M. **Price**.

January 14, 1876 (Continued)

A large number of relatives and friends witnessed the interesting ceremony and enjoyed the festivities. The groom is the son of Mr. Wm. A. **Singleton** of this county, and the bride is a grand daughter of Mrs. F.G. **Gaylord** of Platte City. THE LANDMARK tenders its warmest congratulations.

January 21, 1876

Matrimonial—

Sloan-Simpson--At the residence of Hon Joseph E. **Merryman,** in Platte City, by Elder W.H. **Williams,** on the 19th inst., Mr. David **Sloan** to Miss Jennie **Simpson**, daughter of the late Preston **Simpson**.

The groom is a popular and enterprising young grocer of Platte City, the bride is one of our most aimiable [sic] and interesting young ladies. A large number of intimate friends assembled at the hospitable residence of Hon. Joseph E. Merryman to witness the interesting event, and to tender their congratulations to the happy couple.

Obituary—

Died—At Farley, in this county, on the 28th of September, 1875, Annette Jackson, daughter of N.J. and Elijah C. **Powell**, aged fourteen months and eighteen days.

Little Annette was as bright, beautiful, intelligent, and interesting a child as ever gladdened the hearts of two fond parents.

Her fatal sickness was an attack of congestion of the brain. What made this heavy affliction weigh heavier on her distracted mother, consisted in the fact that the husband and father was at the time, prostrated on what proved to be his death bed, and the heart-rendering prospect of being bereaved of both husband and child, was more than she could bear, and over tasked nature gave way; and such utter prostration and abandonment to grief, I hope I may never be called upon to witness again.

January 21, 1876 (Continued)

On the morning of the day she died, her mother had little Nettie in her arms, when she manifested a desire to be carried to her father's bedside, and upon being taken there, she kissed him passionately all over his wasted face already stamped with the seal of coming death, and on turning away she stretched forth her little hand and said, "Bye, pa, bye, bye," and never spoke again. Sympathizing friends gathered in, to perform the last sad offices for the departed, and some endeavored to point the bereaved mother to the Lamb of God, who has said, "Suffer little children to come unto me," but she, like Rachael, refused to be comforted, because her little one was not. When the time came that all that was mortal of little Nettie must be consigned to the silent chambers of the grave, a long procession of friends and relatives set out to the last resting place, and there the coffin was opened that all who wished, might take a last look and a lesson from the still and pale face within. A smile of heavenly peace seemed to part the tiny mouth, as if even in the last agonies of death she had recognized the bright robed angels waiting to guide her through the infinite regions of space.

[Tribute not copied]

It was deemed appropriate, as she was named after the illustrious and im-mortal Stonewall Jackson, to sing at the grave a hymn composed in honor of the brave old General, whose closing lines, "Let us pass over the river and rest under the shade of the trees," were his own last dying words; also another, a great favorite of the deceased, "Over on the other side," after which the coffin was lowered into the vault, and dust heaped upon dust, and Nettie was left to sleep in her narrow home, till the last trumpet shall call to the sleeping nations, awake ye dead and come to judgment. Peace to the little Nettie.

[Tribute not copied]

January 28, 1876

Married—

JONES—ALLIN

At the residence of the bride's father, Major **Allin,** by Rev. Joseph **Devlin,** on the ___ inst., Mr. John **Jones** to Miss Dulcy D. **Allin**. May their pathway be as a shining light—Joseph **Devlin**.

January 28, 1876

LEWIS—COLLINS

At the residence of the bride's parents in Platte City by Eld. J. B. **McClary**, on the 25th inst, Mr. William **Lewis** to Miss Mary E. **Collins**, daughter of Mr. John **Collins**, all of this county.

We bespeak for the happy pair a prosperous and blissful future, whose pathway through life may be strewn with bright buds of promise and sheltered from the rough storms incident to a terrestial pilgrimage.

February 4, 1876

Obituary—

Died at Farley, October 16th, 1875, of hypertrophy of the heart, Elijah C. **Powell**, aged 62 years and 3 days.

Mr. **Powell** was born in Scott county, Kentucky, the 13th of October, 1813, and removed to this State in 1840, and has been for many years a prominent and influential citizen of this place. The tenor of his whole life has been strongly marked by certain characteristics inherent in his nature. Of a warm-hearted, excitable, nervous temperament, he was very prudent and cautious to a remarkable degree. He was a true and steadfast friend, and a fearless and open enemy to wrong and immorality.

His great regret on his deathbed was that he had not earlier sought for pardon from his pitying Saviour for all his sins. He talked constantly about how good the Lord had been to him in raising him up so many warm friends in the time of need.

Upon being asked if he felt that all was well with him, he replied that "All is well, I know that my Redeemer liveth, and is able and willing to do all He has promised and I shall soon see him face to face and he often urged his friends and family to meet him in heaven; and he remarked upon the shortness and the vanity of life, and often spoke of absent friends, giving messages of love for them. He had lost a little babe by death, a few weeks before, and in speaking of her he said he knew she would meet him at the gates of heaven and welcome him into his eternal rest and in every possible manner left a bright testimony behind him of the power of religion. Never a doubt of shrinking, not a fearful thought, but everything indicated that he had obtained that peace which passeth understanding, which the world can neither give nor take away. At his earnest request he was received into the M.E. Church South, the Rev George [_?_] of Parkville, officiating;

February 4, 1876 (Continued)

and truly that was a solemn scene, one which can never fade from the memory. And when the sacred emblems of the broken body and shed blood were administered, we thought of what our Saviour said upon a similar occasion "Verily I say unto you, I will drink no more of the fruit of the vine, made that day that I drink it anew in the Kingdom of God." He retained his mental faculties clear and bright to the last, and in the midst of such acute suffering, as seldom falls to the lot of man. He was cheerful and resigned willing to bear with patience and resignation whatever the Lord saw in his wisdom and mercy to [?] out to him, and yet willing and anxious to go when the summons should come to call him from earthly life and its trials to that rest that remains to the people of God. So passed away another one of our ancient landmarks. He was the last of the old generation of **Powells** and left a wife and three children to mourn for him. May they take the warning in time and prepare to meet him in that bright world above, where we shall know, even as we are known beyond the shores of time, in which the clouds and gloom that now obscure our pathway, shall be forever dispelled by the glorious effulgence of that God who clothes himself with light as with a garmet is the prayer of their humble friend. S.E. **Depp**

Death of Hon. Thomas Herndon—

Just as we were going to press on Thursday of last week we received information of the death of Hon. Thomas **Herndon**, at his late residence in this city, and were of course precluded from making any extended notice of the fact. Mr. **Herndon** was one of the oldest citizens of Platte City and Platte County, having come here in 1849 and having resided here continuously ever since. He was a native of Madison County, Kentucky and was about fifty-six years old. He came to this place a young lawyer and at once entered upon the practice of his profession, and by industry, application, honesty and integrity established a good practice which he retained until within the last few years. He was not a brilliant lawyer, but he was a painstaking and prudent counselor, and no man ever lived and died in Platte County whose reputation for honesty was better. He was active in politics, laboring always with untiring zeal for his friends and his party, yet he never asked for an office for himself and always declined the pre [?] honors of his party. He was utterly without malice or revengeful feelings and was generous to a fault.

In 1870 his estimable wife died after which he acquired that lamentable habit which in part destroyed his usefulness and hastened his death. He leaves two interesting little daughters who will be cared for by Mrs. **Baker** of Buchanan county, a sister of Mr. **Herndon**. His estate which is practically [?] is worth perhaps about $20,000, and consists chiefly of valuable Platte county lands.

February 4, 1876 (Continued)

Many old friends who had been associated with him for many years accompanied his remains to their final resting place. Let us drop the [_antle] of charity over his faults and only remember the shining virtues of Thomas **Herndon**.

February 11, 1876

Camden Point, Mo February 8, 1876

We are grieved to announce the death of little Willie **Clay**, son of Rev. J. **Clay** which occurred on the evening of February 5th. He was a bright and loveable child and his death is a sad blow to his affectionate parents. Bro. **Clay** and wife have the warmest sympathies of the entire community.

Died—At his late residence, Feb 1, 1876, near Waldron, Mo, Mr. Ignatius **Naylor**, in the 72d year of his age.

The death of Mr. **Naylor** demands more than a simple announcement. He was a native of Kentucky and resided in Platte County for the last twenty-five years, and was well known in this community. All who knew him respected him for his quiet, modest and sincere bearing and character. His death has left a void in his own family, in this community and in society. His devoted heart, his consistent Christian life, his deeds and words of love, have diffused a fragrance around his memory, which will embalm it in the recollection of surviving friends. While his heart clung with natural and fraternal affection to his family and relatives, yet he meekly and submissively obeyed the summons. His remains were committed to the earth far away from his earthly home, but his spirit is with those he loved on earth, now in paradise.

Friday, March 3, 1876

Married at Independence, Mo January 25th, by Elder A.E. **Higgason**, Mr. Walter N. **Woods**, of Jackson County to Miss Eudalia T. **Lampton** of Platte County.

Birth's, Death's and Marriages from the Platte City Missouri "Landmark"

Friday, March 3, 1876 (Continued)

Died—William **Bywaters**, son of J.O. **Bywaters** died near Camden Point on last Wednesday morning, after a very brief illness of pneumonia. He was about twenty-one years old, a sober, moral, upright young man, greatly beloved by all who knew him.

Obituary—

Died—Mrs. Julia **McEowen**, on the 24th, of February, 1876, six miles east of Platte City, Mo.

"I heard a voice from heaven saying unto me, Write; blessed are the dead which die in the Lord from henceforth; Yes, saith the spirit, that they may rest from their labors, and their works do follow them." If this be true-and it is, then is mother **McEowen** truly blessed.

She was born near Philadelphia, Penn, in the year 1809. She joined the church-Old-side Baptist-in the year 1840, in which she lived a pious and useful life, until her master called her from the pain and sorrow of earth to Heaven. "I go," said Christ, "to prepare a place for you. And if I go and prepare a place for you, I will come again, and receive you to myself, that where I am, there ye may be also." She came to Mo., and settled in Platte County about the year 1838. In social life she was a women of few words, but they were words of wisdom and truth. She was of a cheerful and happy spirit, and made all happy around her.

Everybody who knew her loved her, and they who knew her best loved her most. Her's was a candid, honest, just, generous, true, noble heart, carrying sunshine with her everywhere.

Before she left this world she said to her friends: "I am not afraid to die, I am ready when Christ shall call to go hence and be at peace" How blessed the righteous in their death. One son had preceded her to the Glory World.

May the God who saved the mother save all the family, and may they at last make an unbroken family in the great family of God in Heaven.

Mrs. Julia **McEowen** is nor more on earth. She left her home on earth for her home blessed home! In Heaven Feb 24th, 1876

[Tribute not copied]

March 31, 1876

Shortridge-Merchant

On the [22d] of February 1876 by Rev Joseph **Devlin**, Mr. W.T. **Shortridge** and Miss Eliza **Merchant**. May the blessing of the great father attend them through life--. J. Devlin

Mercy-Miller

March 26th, 1876 by Rev John A. **Beagle**. Mr. George R. **Mercy** and Miss Mary A.E. **Miller**.

Died—

--Mr. Benjamin **Kimsey**, one of the oldest citizens of the county died at his residence near Hampton on the 25th ult.

--On Sunday evening at three o'clock Susan H **Wade**, wife of John W. **Wade** of Edgerton, Missouri and daughter of Jacob and Virginia **Creek**. Mrs. **Wade** was born January 8, 1841 and married March 19, 1863, and died March 19, 1876. She united herself with the Baptist church in the year 1855, living strictly up to the rules of the church, and died in the full assurance of a better world leaving a husband and four children, besides many friends and relatives to mourn her loss—A friend

Friday, April 7, 1876

Died:

We regret to announce the death of Blanche, the little daughter of Mr. And Mrs. F.G. **Cockrill**, of membranous croup, which sad event occurred last Saturday evening. The little sufferer was eleven months and seven days old. In their deep affliction Mr. And Mrs. **Cockrill** have the sympathy of the entire community.

At the residence of her husband, on the 31st ult., Mrs. Jennie **Lampton**, wife of Mr. John **Lampton**, aged nineteen years.

Friday, April 14, 1876

Married:

Magers-Crowbarger

At the residence of the bride's mother, two miles northwest of Platte City, April 10th 1875, by Rev D.F. **Bone**, Mr. Lewis C. **Magers** to Miss Cattie M. **Crowbarger**.

> *"Together may they sweetly live*
> *together may they die*
> *Each a starry crown receive*
> *And reign above the sky"*
> ---D.F. **Bone**

April 21, 1876

Died at his residence in Platte County near Union Mills, Mr. Alex **Horn**, aged about sixty five years

Married: At the residence of Paisley **Johnson**, in Buchanan County, by Rev. Vincent **Jones**, on the 9th inst, Joseph H. **Pumphrey** of Platte county to Miss Sue **Sherwood** of Buchanan county.

We congratulate our young friends and sincerely hope that their wedded lives may be as happy as our skies are fair.

At the residence of the bride's parents on the 13th inst by Rev Jeramiah **Clay**, Mr. Joseph **Monzey** to Miss Annie **Warren**, both of Platte County

April 28, 1876

Died in the Penitentiary-

Archibald **Hill**, for several years postmaster at Ridgley in this county, and convicted about four years ago of tampering with the mails, and sentenced for ten years in the penitentiary, died in prison on the 12th of this month. He was about sixty-five years of age.

Married—on the 25th inst by Rev D.F. **Bone** at the residence of the officiating pastor in Platte City, Mr. Joseph C. [**Jamis**] of Abilene, Kansas to Miss Bettie C. **McNemar** of Platte County.

Died: Died in Platte County on the 23d inst, Mrs. Anna, wife of William E. **Minor**. The funeral services were conducted by Elder **Wyatt**. Mrs. Minor nee **Greeg**, was a sister of Mrs. **Edgar**, formerly of St. Joseph, and of Mrs. J. B. **Dean** of Platte County, and leaves a large connection to mourn her loss.

June 2, 1876

A Notable Marriage—On Tuesday morning May 24, 1876, Mr. William H. **Armstrong** and Miss Clara **Almond** were married by Rev Oren **Root**, President of Pritchett's Institute, at the Presbyterian Church in Glasglow, Mo. Mr. **Armstrong** is a wealthy and influential citizen of Glasglow, and his bride is one of the fairest and most gifted young ladies of the state. She is daughter of the late Judge W.B. **Almond** of Platte City, and was born and reared in our community. Her father was one of the most distinguished men of the state in his day, having been honored with high judicial and political positions both in this state and in California. The family was justly celebrated for his high social standing and its women for their beauty, culture, and grace. Miss Clara inherited in a marked degree all the characteristics of her patrician lineage and her friends and admirers in her old Platte county home are numbered by scores, and every one will waft her a bon voyage in her matrimonial enterprise. We learn from the journal that the wedded couple immediately departed for the Centennial.

Birth's, Death's and Marriages from the Platte City Missouri "Landmark"

June 2, 1876 (Continued)

Died—

Mrs. America R. **Perry**, wife of Charles E. **Perry**, in this city at 11 o'clock a.m. on the [23d] day of May.

Mrs. **Perry** was 32 years of age, the daughter of Col. James **Hamilton** of Lebanon, Tenn. She was a member of the Methodist church and a true Christian lady. She leaves a large circle of mourning relatives and friends. Her funeral will take place today, the 24th instant, from the family residence—*Jefferson City Journal*

June 9, 1876

Died on the [?] inst. At her residence is Parkwell, Platte County, Mo. Mrs.[Jille] F., wife of Mr. C.H. **Taylor** in the 33rd year of her age.

The deceased had been lingering for near five months, with an incurable disease. She leaves a stricken husband and an only child, a little daughter aged eight years to mourn their sad loss. May the good Shepard guard and protect them.

June 16, 1876

A Brilliant Wedding—

Thursday evening, June 15th, Mr. Girard **Chestnut**, deputy sheriff of Platte county, and Miss Lida F. **Park**, daughter of Mr. Simpson **Park**, were married at the residence of the latter, near Platte City. The attendants were Mr. E. **Chestnut**, of St. Joseph and Miss Rosa **Kirch**, of Leavenworth, and Mr. John **Morin** and Miss Amanda **Dillingham**, of Platte County. The ceremony was performed by Eld J.B. **McCleary**, of Leavenworth in a most impressive manner. A large number of the immediate friends and relatives of the contracting parties were present, and many valuable presents were displayed.

June 16, 1876 (Continued)

The bride is beautiful, highly educated and accomplished. The groom is one of the rising young men of Platte County, justly celebrated for his excellent qualities of head and heart. THE LANDMARK'S best wishes go with the happy pair through life.

An elegant reception takes place at Capt. **Chestnut's** today

June 30, 1876

Married—

Berger—Knopf

On Saturday evening last, the ceremonies were performed at the Presbyterian Church in Platte City, which united the above.
"Two hearts that beat as one"
in the holy bonds of matrimony. The happy pair were Mr. Julius **Berger**, of Leavenworth and Mrs. Victoria **Knopf**, of Platte City. How the affair was brought about we are unable to report. It was supposed by **Berger's** friends that he was matrimonial proof, but it seems that he never heard the advice of the elder weller "Bevare of the vidders," consequently his capture. For our part we are glad he is captured. He has secured a charming wife, and one that can render home happy. The *Appeal* heartily congratulates the happy pair, and trusts the bridegroom may never feel the need of a button when he wants to use one.—*Leavenworth Appeal*

Married—

At Junction City, Oregon, by Rev E.R. **Geary**, May 30th, 1876, Mr. John **Somerville** and Miss Ellen **Brasfield**, late of Platte county, Missouri.

A few months ago Miss **Brasfield**, who is a daughter of the late T.W. R. **Brasfield**, and niece of Judge John S. **Brasfield**, of this county, went to Oregon on a visit to relatives and friends. It appears from the above announcement that she soon became entangled in Cupid's meshes and is now a happy bride. Her husband, we learn, is a wealthy and influential citizen of his section, and is proud of his conquest. He is, of course, a stranger to us, but we cannot refrain from congratulating him upon securing for a life companion one of the purest and truest of womankind, and for her and hers THE LANDMARK has nothing but good wishes. May their lives be long and happy.

July 7, 1876

A Centennial Wedding—

A Novel and pleasant event at the Fourth of July celebration at Weston was the public marriage of Mr. John **Anderson** and Miss Lucy C. **Sowder**. They were escorted to the grand stand by their friends, Messrs. W. H. **Ballard** and Dr. **Shortridge**, masters of ceremonies, and then, in the presence of thousands of people, Rev. J.A. **Beagle** performed the marriage ceremony. The band played the wedding march and congratulations were freely bestowed.

Obituary—

Mrs. Jennie **Lampton** died at the residence of her husband near Second Creek Church, Platte County, on the [_1st_] of March, 1876, being 19 years, 5 months and 13 days of age.

The deceased was the daughter of Mr. And Mrs. E. J. **Link**, and about a year and a half ago was united in marriage to Mr. John **Lampton**, whom she now leaves disconsolate to mourn his great loss. She leaves an interesting little boy behind, together with a large circle of relatives and friends. She was a worthy and acceptable member of the Christian Church of more than three years standing, and died triumphantly, admonishing her friends to live consistent Christian lives and meet her "just over there." How the heart aches, when friends are cut down in the springtime of life, and all our cherished hopes are crushed in a moment But:

> There is a Divinity that shapes our ends
> [_____ as we may]

July 14, 1876

Boy Drowned—

Last Saturday, about 2 o'clock P.M., William **Cole**, aged about fifteen years, son of Mr. James **Cole**, nephew of Mr. David **Cole** living a few miles south of Platte City, was drowned under the following circumstances. In company with several other boys about the same age he went in bathing just below the mill dam, near town. Young **Cole** was a poor swimmer, and stepping off a ledge of rocks into deep water, mad a few ineffectual struggles and sank. The alarm was speedily given, and unceasing efforts were made to recover the body. During the afternoon, and all night, and all day and all night Sunday,

July 14, 1876 (Continued)

parties were at work dragging the river, diving, firing cannons and resorting to all the usual expedients under similar circumstances. But the body was not found until Monday morning, when it was discovered lodged in a drift about a mile down the river. It was taken out, coffined and borne to its last resting place in the family burying ground. It was truly a lamentable accident, and much sympathy is freely expressed for the family of the deceased.

July 28, 1876

Married—At Camden Point, Mo., by Rev. Jeremiah **Clay**, on the 20th inst., Mr. John W. **Jack** and Miss Lou **Parrish**, both of Platte County.

We congratulate our young friends over this happy consummation and wish them abundant success in life.

Married—at the residence of the bride's parents, near Little Rock, Ark., Mr. J.A. **Hudson** of Little Rock, to Miss Lizzie E. **McKinnis**, by the Rev. A.R. **Wenfield**, of Red Bluff, Ark. No date given.

August 4, 1876

Death of An Aged Lady.—On the 24th ult. Mrs. Spicey **Lanter** died at the residence of her son Sidney **Lanter**, at Farley in this county, after a long and distressing illness of dropsy. Mrs. **Lanter**, whose maiden name was **Davis**, was born in Madison County, Kentucky, February 16th, 1800, and was, therefore at the time of her death in her seventy seventh year. She and her husband Thomas **Lanter** removed to Howard county, Mo., thence to Clay and finally to Platte in 1842, where she has ever since resided, honored and respected by all who knew her. She was the mother of eleven children, seven of whom are yet living, among whom are Capt. Davis and Sidney **Lanter** and Mrs. Robert **Carson**. Many years ago Mrs. **Lanter** united with the Christian Church, being baptized by Elder Oliver **Steele**, and has been a consistent member ever since. She was a woman of great force of character and has left her impress upon the community in which she lived. She was buried last Tuesday in the old Green burying ground, a large concourse of old friends, neighbors and relatives following her remains to their final resting place. Rev. D.F. **Bone** conducted the religious services. Having passed beyond the allotted years of most persons, she fell asleep perfectly resigned and assuredly trustful of the future.

Married—

July 26th 1876, at the residence of Mr. James **Flannery** in Platte City, Mo, By Rev D.F. **Bone**, Mr. Auscar **Brown**, of DeKalb county, to Miss Kattic **Kuykendall** of Platte county, Mo.

Killed By lightening—

The people of this section of country will remember the wind and rain storm last Friday night. It was during that war of the elements that Charles **Snyder**, a young man of twenty-eight, was killed by a bolt of lightening. He was at the residence of the widow **Beery**, two miles north of Smithville. He was standing in the door when the lightening struck the house and passed down the stovepipe. Passing out, it struck Mr. **Snyder** on the head, tearing a large piece of the scalp off, passed down his right side to his foot, when it tore open his boot leg and passed to the floor. Mr. **Snyder** fell back dead in the midst of the horror-stricken family. Several other persons were stunned but not severely injured.

Birth's, Death's and Marriages from the Platte City Missouri "Landmark"

August 11, 1876

Death Of An Estimable Lady—

Mrs. Matilda E. **Link**, wife of Mr. David J. **Link**, died at the family residence about seven miles east of Platte City last Friday afternoon. Her death was so sudden as to startle the whole community. About 1 o'clock Friday morning she was suddenly taken with a violent spell of phthysic, a disease to which she had been somewhat subject. She continued to grow worse, and during the day congestion of the lungs supervened and at 3 o'clock P.M. she died.

Mrs. **Link** was the daughter of the late B.L. **Lampton**, of Clay county, and was born March 11th, 1830, and was married November 23d, 1847. In 1854 she united with the Christian Church, and ever afterwards faithfully followed the precepts of the divine master. Her husband and four children survive her, and to them the deepest sympathy is extended. In all the relations of life Mrs. **Link** filled her allotted part conscientiously and nobly. She was a faithful wife, a devoted mother, an earnest Christian, and as a neighbor and member of society was a woman beloved by all and whose home was the abode of cheerfulness and happiness.

Died—

Mr. Luther **Teegarden**, of Weston, died last Saturday evening, aged about seventy-five years. He was one of our oldest and most valued citizens.

Married—

At the residence of G. W. **Fields**, New Market, Platte county, on the 3d inst., by Elder W. C. **Rogers**, Mr. J. L. **Cormack** to Miss Deede **Fields**.

Attendants, M. William **McGeorge** and Miss Laura B. **Gabbert**.

It was a quiet, unpretentious affair, but one the less pleasant to those who were there. Mr. Cormack is a popular young lawyer; his bride is beautiful, amiable and intelligent, so congratulations are due both.

As down the stream of life they float
May skies be blue above them;
No storm to darken o'er their way.
But softest breezes move them;
And flowers to fill the enchanted way
With sweetest perfumes o'er;
No tears but such as come from joy,
And love and hope forever.

Birth's, Death's and Marriages from the Platte City Missouri "Landmark"

August 18, 1876

Married-- at the residence of the bride's Father, James **Ratliff**, August 15, 1876, by Rev D.F. **Bone**, Mr. John H. **Flishman** and Miss Matilda **Ratliff**, all of Platte County.

August 26, 1876

Obituary—

Mrs. Matilda E. **Link**, wife of David **Link**, died at her residence in Platte, County, Mo. August 4th, 1876, of congestion of the lungs, in the 47th year of her age.

She was born in Clark County, Kentucky, March 11th, 1830. While she was yet young her parents removed to Clay County, Mo., where she was married to her now bereaved husband on the 23^{d} of November, 1847. In the year of 1864 she united with the Christian Church at Second Creek, in which communion she lived and died, useful and highly esteemed by all who knew her.

She was a good wife, a faithful and loving mother and a devoted Christian. Her last sickness was violent, brief and painful, but borne with Christian patience and resignation. She was taken violently about 1 o'clock in the morning and expired about half-past three in the afternoon. Conversing with her husband a short time before her death she expressed a willingness, if it was the will of God, to depart and be with Christ. Her greatest regret was to leave him and her children, requesting him to take charge of them and raise them in the nurture and admonition of the Lord. Her husband and four children, her mother and a large circle of acquaintances and friends constituted the [ ] of mourners who followed her remains to the grave at Second Creek Church. But they sorrow not as those having no hope. She has gone to her reward. Peace to her memory. We sympathize with her bereaved family, and pray that God in his providence may keep them pure and upright until they meet the loved one among the marshaled hosts of heaven where parting will be no more.

Birth's, Death's and Marriages from the Platte City Missouri "Landmark"

September 8, 1876

Married—A pleasant party of the relatives and friends of Mr. John **Dillingham** and Miss Annie **Oldham**, assembled on Tuesday evening, Aug, 31st at the residence of Mr. F. M. **Oldham**, near Platte City to witness the solemnization of their nuptials. The ceremony was preformed by Rev. D.F. **Bone**, pastor of the Methodist church, in a brief but very impressive manner. The attendants were Miss Lula **Pitt** and Mr. George **Mason**. The bride, one of the most beautiful, intelligent and loveable young ladies of our community, was dressed with exquisite style and bore herself with a modest grace and dignity that evoked the admiration of all. The groom was a self possessed and as happy as a prince come late into the possession of heritage. After the congratulations, which were joyous and heart-felt, had been extended, the assembled guests were invited to the dining room, where a rare collection of cakes, wines, fruits, ices and confections awaited them, and to which ample justice was done. Mr. And Mrs. **Oldham**, by their open-hearted hospitality, made everybody happy. After the banquet, the hours were beguiled away with music and pleasant conversation, and all departed, bearing with them good wishes for the happy pair. Among those present, we noticed Mr. And Mrs. R.T. **Darnall**, Mr. And Mrs. W. O. **Oldham**, Judge **Chiles** and lady, Prof, **Gaylord** and Mr. Simpson **Park**, besides a large number of young ladies and gentlemen. On Friday night, the bridal party held a reception at Mr. Elisha **Dillingham's** which was a very pleasant affair and largely attended.

Suicide—

Last Friday Mr. James **Hamilton**, a highly respectable citizen of the neighborhood of New Market, disappeared from his home under circumstances that justified the gravest suspicions concerning his intentions. Not returning, search was instituted without avail until Monday evening, when he was found hanged to a limb of a tree not far from his home. It was and evident case of suicide resulting from a temporarily degraded intellect. Mr. **Hamilton** was a brother of Mr. John **Hamilton** and brother-in-law of Mr. W.G. **Cox** and Mr. I.P. **Cartwright**. He was a man of excellent standing in the community in which he lived, and his untimely end causes intense grief among his friends. There was no apparent cause for the rash act.

Birth's, Death's and Marriages from the Platte City Missouri "Landmark"

September 22, 1876

A Good Citizen Dead—

Mr. F.H. **Ohlschlager**, a leading German citizen living near Farley, died last Saturday, aged forty-five years, after a very brief illness. This news will be a painful surprise to the many friends of Mr. **Ohlschlager** throughout the county. Mr. O was born in northern Germany and has been a resident of Platte County about ten years. His influence in his neighborhood was unlimited and was always exerted for the good of his neighbors and the welfare of the county. He was a fine businessman, and a live, enterprising citizen, despising hypocrisy and deceit, and loving honesty and fair dealing. Truly Platte County has lost a good citizen. Mr. **Ohlschlager** leaves five children, who fortunately have a competence and friends to care for them.

Death of an Aged Lady—

It is with exceeding pain that the sad intelligence of the death of Mrs. Catherine **Foley** will be read by the many relations and friends of the deceased at the home of her son-in-law and daughter, Mr. And Mrs. J. **Clifford**, at Tracy, Platte county, Mo, at 1 o'clock, on the morning of the 17th inst. The deceased was born in County Kerry, Ireland, Feb 1st, 1787, and was consequently, at the time of her death 89 years, 7 months, and 10 days old. She had resided with Mr. And Mrs. J. **Clifford** for the past twenty years, to whom she has been endeared by her many sots of kindness and liberality. She was a resident of Platte county for the past nineteen years, seven of them being in the immediate neighborhood of Platte City. As a mother she was loving, and as a strict member of her Church she distinguished herself by the holy and edifying life she led. Her remains were entombed in the city cemetery at Weston.

Married—

At the residence of the bride's father, Mr. Drury **Willis**, by Eld. A. F. **Smith**, on the 19th inst., Mr. William C. **Harlan** and Miss M. J. **Willis**—all of Platte county.

October 6, 1876

Married—

On the 3d inst. at the Christian Church, in this city at 8 1/2 o'clock A.M., by Eld. T.N. **Gaines** of Richmond, Mo, Mr. Joseph **McKee** of Lawson, Ray County Mo to Miss Katie **Bullingsworth** of this place. We bespeak for the wedded pair a life full of happiness and may their voyage to the final goal be full of that frutation, the ultimate Thule of mans greatest ambition.

October 13, 1876

An infant son of Mr. Paul **Shepard** died last Saturday.

Mrs. **Duncan**, mother-in-law of Mr. John **Thatcher**, died near Smithville last week, aged about eighty years.

Died—

On the 10th inst., at the residence of her grandmother, Mrs. Delilah **Baber**, Elizabeth Ann **Kimsey**, aged eighteen, daughter of W. H. and E.A. **Kimsey**.

Birth's, Death's and Marriages from the Platte City Missouri "Landmark"

October 13, 1876 (Continued)

Married—

At the residence of Mr. Robt. **Rose**, near Iatan, by A.G. **Smith**, Esquire, on the 10th inst., Mr. Richard **Pemberton** to Miss Ollie **Kidwell**, all of Platte County.

Dr. Willis Bledsoe—The death of Dr. Willis **Bledsoe**, at Farley, last week, a brief mention of which was made in THE LANDMARK, deserves more than a passing notice. Dr. **Bledsoe** held a place in the hearts of the people with whom he lived that no other man can fill. He was warmhearted and generous to an extent that always kept him poor in this world's goods, but rich in the affections of men. In his community his self-imposed mission was to visit the sick, care for those in distress and serve his friends. A good man has fallen. Peace to his ashes.

Mrs. Ann Oliver--, Widow of the late William E. **Oliver**, died at her residence in this city last Friday. She leaves five children, who are fortunately well provided for by the kindness of relatives and friends.

October 20, 1876

Married at Waldron, on the 16th inst, by Esquire **Flynn**. James Henry **Nowland** to Miss Sidney Jane **Dunagan**, both of Waldron.

October 27, 1876

Died—

At the residence of the parents, east of Platte City, on the 16th inst., of membranous croup, Lizzie Henderson, daughter of Capt. James and Jane **Synnamon**, aged fifteen months.

News has just been received here of the death of Mr. Logan B. **Lampton**, formerly of this county, at Missouri City, on the 12 inst. His wife, Nee Miss Sallie **Akers**, died about one month before. An obituary notice is promised for nest week's issue of THE LANDMARK.

Obituary—

Tempie—Died near New Market, October 17, 1876, only child of Abe and Flora **Purrin**, aged eleven days.

The little one has been transplanted in the heavenly country before sin had laid its blighting touch upon her. How weak we are, dear Flora, to mourn the departure of the little one, when we are assured that "of such is the kingdom of heaven." Jesus loves little children. Little Tempie has gone to live with the angels and purifies spirits in that beautiful place that JESUS has gone to prepare. Weep not for the loved one; she is not dead, she is now, we trust, enjoying the companionship of our dear Mother. Let us not murmur, but bow submissively to the will of Him who is able to bring us face to face with the loved ones He has taken away. –Janie Camden Point, Oct 22, 1876.

--We record the death of Mr. Obediah **Timberlake** of this place, who died on the 19th last, aged 36 years. The funeral was attended at the house on the 20th. The remains were taken to the Naylor graveyard for interment.

Birth's, Death's and Marriages from the Platte City Missouri "Landmark"

November 3, 1876

Married

On Oct. 24th, 1876, at Mt. Vernon Church in this county by Rev. Cad **Lewis**, Mr. Kemp M. **Woods** Jr., of Clay County, Mo., to Miss Lillie M. **Wigglesworth** of Woodford.

Missouri has plucked another byd from our Woodford parterre, and this time our loveliest *Lily* adorns her *Woods*. We have rarely parted with a young lady so beautiful and accomplished, but it is gratifying to know that she is entrusted to deserving and careful hands. Mr. **Woods** is not entirely a stranger, his father having been a native and long a worthy citizen of Woodford County.

After receiving the congratulations of their friends the happy pair left for the bridal tour including the Centennial and other points of interest, after which they will return to their Missouri home. May all happiness and good fortune attend them. -- *Woodford (Ky.) Weekly.*

Weston Items:

--Mrs. Lou **Kitchen**, wife of Mr. Geo. **Kitchen**, died near Edgerton on Tuesday of last week.

--Mrs. Phebe **Graves** died, near Weston on the 20th ult.

--Mr. John **Bigham**, of Platte county, and Miss E. J. **Davis**, of Buchanan county, were married at DeKalb on the 15th ult.

November 10, 1876

Obituaries of Mr. and Mrs. Logan B. Lampton

Logan B. **Lampton** died of pulmonary phtindid, at his residence in Missouri City, Clay County. Mo., October 12th, 1876, being a little over 27 years of age.

He was the son of Beverly T. **Lampton** and was born in Cooper county, Mo., September 16, 1819. When a child he removed with his parents to Platte County.

Here he chiefly received his education, and in August 1866, joined the Christian Church at Second Creek Church in Platte county. In which he lived a worthy and consistent member until called from his earthly pilgrimage. October 20, 1870, he was married to Miss Sallie **Aker**, daughter of Elder Preston **Aker**, who but a short time before preceded him to world of spirits. He leaves behind him three small children, two sons and a daughter, and two brothers and five sisters to mourn his early demise and premature decay. He chose teaching for a profession, and having qualified himself for its duties, spent several years in this vocation in the public schools of Platte and Clay counties. He was modest and diffident in demeanor, but affable and pleasant in his social relations, and firm and consistent and faithful in his Christian life. During his protracted illness he often expressed his willingness to die, and the confident assurance which he had of soon being with his dear Christian wife, who but thirty days before had crossed over the flood, and was reposing in the shadow of the trees in the happy "Summer Land" beyond.

This affliction leaves a deep gloom hanging over his family, and crushed and mangled hearts bleeding from sad bereavement; but they mourn not as those who have no hope. "To live is gain; but to die, and be with Christ, is far better."

Mrs. Sallie **Lampton**, wife of L.B. **Lampton** and daughter of Elder Preston **Aker**, died in a congestive chill, at the residence of her husband, in Missouri City, Clay county, Mo., September 12th 1876, being twenty-five years and twenty six days of age.

The subject of this notice was born in Platte County, Mo., August 16th, 1851. She united with the Christian church at Smithville, Clay County, in July, 1865, and during the remainder of her life shed forth the fragrance of a meek, patient, Christian spirit. October 20th of 1870 she was united in marriage with Mr. Logan B. **Lampton**, who in one short month after her decease, followed her to the spirit world. How inscrutable are the ways of the just and infinate Parent, "who maketh the clouds his chariot, his ministers a flame of fire." Educated and endowed with many accomplishments, she surrounded herself with many fast friends, who now with sorrowing hearts keenly feel how great and irreparable is their loss. Seized and held in the icy arms of the fatal congestion, she was buried into eternity without one moment's warning, an admonition to all her friends to "be ye also ready." But she is now emancipated from the sorrows and sufferings of earth,

November 10, 1876 (Continued)

and admitted to the city with "many mauelous," "whither the forerunner for us has entered," and from which death is forever banished.

We breathe the sincere prayer that God may ever provide ample friends for their three hapless children.

November 17, 1876

A Sad Bereavement—

Last Wednesday, Nov. 15th, 1876, Willie C. **Park**, son of Mr. Jefferson J. and Mattie **Park**, aged 20 years, 6 moths and 18 days, died of inflammation of the bowels, at the family residence, four miles east of Platte City, and was buried at Platte City yesterday, Elder A.F. **Smith** conducting the funeral exercises.

Willie was a bright, intelligent and amiable young man, just in the morning of life, with a promising future before him and a host of friends to love and encourage him. His untimely end will cast a gloom over many hearts and start a tear of sympathy for his afflicted parents and brothers and sister.

Married—

At the residence of the bride's mother, on Nov. 9th, 1876 by the Rev. D. F. **Bone**, Mr. T. K. **Eskridge** to Miss Louisa **Bane**, all of Platte County, Mo.

The attendants were Miss Fannie **Oliver** and Mr. Jno. O. **Yates** and Miss Mattie **Phillips** and Mr. Thornton **Coons**. A large number of kindred and friends were present to do the happy pair honor and the magnificent supper justice. May Heaven's choicest blessings rest with this happy pair.

--D.F.B.

December 8, 1876

We learn with extreme regret that Dr. Wm. A. **Brock** is lying dangerously ill at the residence of Judge **Owens** near Camden Point. Dr. **Brock** was a prominent physician of St. Joseph and had to abandon his profession a few months ago on account of his failing health.

Since the above was written we learn that dr. **Brock** has died.

Married—from cards received we learn that Mr. Frank F. **Todd**, of St. Joseph and Miss Dorcas H. **Owen**, of Eminence, Ky., were married in the Christian Church at the latter place December 6th last Wednesday.

Frank is a Platte county boy and here, as everywhere, he has a host of warm friends who waft to him the most earnest congratulations. May all the future of their lives glow with the warmest light of love and may peace and prosperity ever attend the happy pair.

December 15, 1876

--Married- Dec. 10, 1876, at the residence of Mrs. Sue **Reneau**, by Rev D.F. **Bone**, Mr. John **Alexander**, to Miss Jennie **Stewart**, all of Platte County, Mo.

May their path be as the shining light, which shineth more and more unto the perfect day.

--**December 12th, 1876**, at the residence of Mrs. Sue **Reneau**, by Rev. D. F. **Bone**, Mr. Silas D. **Morgan** to Mrs. Sue D. **Reneau**, all of Platte county, Mo.

There were present to witness the nuptial ceremonies A. R. **Demasters**, Grundy **Cockrill**, Mrs. Elizabeth **Tribble**, Giles **Owens** and a few others, who heartily congratulated the happy couple, wishing them a long and happy life. We do heartily wish that no dark cloud may ever obscure the bright heaven of their love. May they ever sing, as doubtless they do this morning.

Birth's, Death's and Marriages from the Platte City Missouri "Landmark"

December 22, 1876

Death of an Aged Lady—

Lucy G. **Silvey** died at the residence of her son, James M. **Silvey**, in this county, on the 9th inst. Mrs. **Silvey** was one of the eldest ladies in the county having been born near Frankfort, Kentucky March 9, [1796]. She was married to James M. **Silvey** in 1812 and removed to St. Charles, Mo. in [1816] and to Platte County in [1840]. Her husband died about thirty years ago. She joined the Christian church in 1853 and was until the day of her death a consistent member thereof. She is the mother of Mrs. Alfred **Owens** and Mr. James M. **Silvey**, of this county. Mrs. **Silvey** was one of the truest and best women of the country and goes to her final rest mourned by all who knew her.

December 29, 1876

Married—Mr. Charles **Harris**, of this county, was married by Elder P. **Aker** at Missouri City on the 21st inst., to Miss Laura **Herron**, of Jackson county.

We are informed that Charley has secured a jewel of a wife and we congratulate him accordingly.

Died—Ruth Ann, daughter of Ben E. and Deborah **Perry**, age nineteen months, died on the 24th inst. And was buried on the 25th. Eld. A. F. **Smith** conducted the funeral ceremonies.

January 5, 1877

Death of Mrs. Anna B. Park

Death is at all times solemn, Even when it gathers to its embrace the aged whose sands of life have run out and whose [___] had been decried by the nature of irrevocable law, there is a sorrowful solemnnility in death. But when the [lusatiate] archer strikes down

January 5, 1877 (Continued)

the young and pure and beautiful then comes to many hearts a sorrow that even time cannot assuage.

On the 21st of December last there died at West Las Animas, away out on the plains of Colorado, Mrs. Anna Bronaugh **Park**, a young women whom two counties in Missouri (Clay and Platte) delighted to claim and to love. She had gone there with her husband John W. **Park**, in search of health and a little longer lease of life which the mountains and plains of Colorado were supposed to give to invalids. She was young loved and loving, with four bright little boys, and a husband who idolized her and friends who loved her with an untold wealth of affection. All that makes life sweet and worth living was hers. But the Death Angel came all the same and claimed the loveliest victim, and from its black wings threw into many hearts the shadow of an immeasurable woe.

Anna Bronaugh was the daughter of John and Hannah **Bronaugh**, an old Virginia family, and was born October 22d, 1844. For two years she was a student at the Platte City Female Academy while that institution was under the control of Prof. Hugh B. Todd. Her beauty, grace, vivacity and intelligence won all hearts and made her a great favorite with all. Her accomplishments were all that wealth and admiring parents could give, and these she exercised in such a manner as to make all love her who came within the range of her gentle influence

In social life she was the centre of a circle of devoted friends and admirers and no social gathering was complete without her presence

About the year 1865 she became a member of the Christian church. In whose communities she lived and died.

On the 28th, of March, 1867, she was married to John W. **Park** of Platte county and immediately afterwards became a resident of Platte County. Four intelligent little boys blessed their union; three of whom were with her at the time of her death.

In the spring of 1875 her sister being prostrated with a fatal illness, Mrs. **Park** became her [____] attendant and was with her night and day, until her death. During this illness she contracted a severe cold, which added to her mental afflictions, cumulated in a pulmonary disease. In the fall of the same year her devoted husband, by the advice of her physician, took her to Golden City, Colorado, where she remained about three months, improving immensely that she thought she could only venture to come home. But from the time she arrived at home she rapidly grew worse and no medical and or loving attention could check the progress of the insidious disease. Therefore In February 1876 her husband took her to Trinidad, Colorado, and in September to West Las Animas All methods of living which had in them the prospect of relief were tried, including [_____] out, housekeeping and a trip through New Mexico. All however was without avail and soon she was prostrated and only a seductive hope remained to cheer her and her family and friends.

January 5, 1877 (Continued)

Multitudes of friends and her mother and [____] administered at her bedside and after bidding all an affectionate farewell and sending loving messages and imparting dying bequests to absent friends, with mind unclouded and perfect resignation, she peacefully sank to rest and life's [____] was over.

Her body was brought to Kansas City, and then taken to her childhood's home in Clay County, where in compliance with her request, it remained over night mid the scenes of her youth, and on the 28th of December was deposited beside the remains of her idolized sister in Barry. The beautiful burial service of the Episcopal Church being performed at her grave.

"Thus passed away in the bloom of youth, Anna B. Park. Words of sympathy for those she left behind are idle for time only, which [____] healing apostle wings can blunt the pain of sorrow and bring blessed resignation. If the rewards of a virtuous and well spent life are made to heaven, then there's a glorious crown for [____]. -Amen

--We are requested to give notice of the death of W. B. **Soper**, which occurred at Houston, Texas, on the 27th of November. It is supposed that Mr. **Soper** has friends and acquaintanences in Platte county.

Married—

--At the residence of the brides father, Mr. John R. **Duncan**, by Rev. D. F. **Bone**, Mr. Marcellus **Stallard** to Miss Isabella **Duncan**, Dec. 27, 1876. The attendants were T. M. **Baughman** and Annie **Duncan**, Wm. **Mcgeorge** and Mary **Arnold**, James **Browning** and lady J. L. **[Carman]** and lady D. R. **Stallard** and lady R. W. **Bywaters** and lady and a host of young people were present to witness the marriage ceremonies to wish the happy couple a long and happy life and to do ample justice to the magnificent repast which was prepared for the occasion.

--**December 28th,** 1876 at the residence of Mr. Henry **Gray**, by the Rev. A. T. **Lewis**, Mr. John W. **Noland** to Miss Sarah A. **Demoss** all of Platte County, Peace, happiness and success in life to this young couple, and in the end, everlasting life.

--**On the 27th day of Dec., 1876**, by Esquire S. M. **Crockett**, at his residence near Ridgely, Mr. Charles **Moore** to Miss Tat **Hunter**, all of Platte county.

Birth's, Death's and Marriages from the Platte City Missouri "Landmark"

January 12, 1877

Died-

Tilden Hendricks **Jacks**, son of C. J. and M. S. **Jacks**, died at the residence of the parents in this county, December 14, 1876, aged three weeks and four days. The sympathies of the community are with Mr. and Mrs. **Jacks** in their bereavement.

Died—

Watson B. **Stitt**, infant son of William and Mary **Stitt**, was born July 18, 1876, and died January 4, 1877 at 9 o'clock and 6 minutes, a.m.

The blessed Christ said, "Suffer little children to come unto me and forbid them not; for such is the Kingdom of God" Often God doubtless calls the little ones to himself that the affections of the parents may be lifted to heaven.

The sweet child [_____] tasted the bitter of this sinful world, then shrank back to the joys of heaven. Yes, this tender bud has faded from earth to bloom in heaven forever. The writer preached the funeral of the child on the 5th of January 1877 at the residence of the parents, amid the might of sympathizing friends. May God bless and sustain by his grace the bereaved parents, and bring them to meet their dear little one where there is no death.

January 26, 1877

A Sudden Death—

We were pained to learn of the bereavement that befel Pro. **Dohart** and his wife of Camden Point. When they retired on Friday night, near 12 o'clock, their infant daughter, ten months of age, appeared to be about in usual health. Her mother's quick eye thought she detected some indication of unusual drowsiness, but not sufficient to create any alarm. But when they awoke next morning, they found to their bitter anguish that their child had passed from life to death. Their loss is the more keenly felt, the more unbearable, on the account of the suddenness of the shock and the mystery that necessarily gathers around the last moments of their little child. They have no means by which they can ascertain its cause of death. Two physicians were called in early as possible, but they were not able to form any opinion—Indeed, they could scarcely reach a vague conjecture. The funeral service was conducted on Sunday in the parlors of the Orphan school. The bereaved father and mother have lost their only daughter in the tender period of babyhood. No one can appreciate what this loss means who has not suffered like them. We offer our warmest sympathy to theme in this hour of their trial.

Birth's, Death's and Marriages from the Platte City Missouri "Landmark"

February 2, 1877

Death of Mrs. Sloan—

Mrs. Mahala **Sloan**, wife of Mr. Allen **Sloan**, died at the family residence, about three miles west of Platte city, of cancer of he breast, on the morning of the 31st ult. Mrs. **Sloan** was one of the best known and most estimable ladies in Platte County, and her unexpected death will be a painful shock to her numerous friends. For many years she lived in Platte city, until the death of her first husband, Dr. **Wallace**, and in 1864 was married to Mr. Allen **Sloan**. She was a devoted member of the Cumberland Presbyterian Church, and lived and died in its communion. We hope to have the data for a fuller notice next week.

The funeral will take place at 10 o'clock today (Friday) from the Presbyterian Church.

February 9, 1877

Wedded-

Last Sunday morning our gallant young friend Mr. M. M. **Miller**, after many years roving, was gathered to the society of the benedicts. This notable event occurred at the residence of Mr. Samuel **Hoy**, and the high contracting parties were Mr. M. M. **Miller** and Miss May **Hoy**. The officiating minister was the Rev. Harry **Foster**, of Leavenworth county, Kansas, and the attendants Mr. W. W. **Bixey** and Miss. Lydia **Hoy**. On the evening of the same day there was a reception at the residence of Capt. W. J. **Miller**, the grooms father, which was attended by a large number of friends and a most enjoyable evening was spent,..

Death of Mrs. Sloan--

Last week we made brief mention of the death of Mrs. **Sloan**, wife of Mr. Allen **Sloan**, of this county. The death of such a women deserves more than a passing notice, for she was known by nearly everybody and beloved by everybody in the county.

Mrs. Mahala Davis **Home**(?) was born in Boonville, Cooper county, Missouri, May 17th, 1823. Her mother survives her, and is living at Boonville at the venerable age of eighty-eight years.

February 9, 1877 (Continued)

She was married to Dr. H. B. **Wallace** September 15, 1846 and with her husband moved to Platte City in 1851. Her husband was one of the most eminent physicians and prominent citizens of the Platte Purchase and their home was the abode of wealth, hospitality and charity. Her husband dying on the 31st of March, 1864, she was married to Mr. Allen **Sloan**, one of Platte county's most honorable and upright citizens.

Mrs. **Sloan** was for twenty-five years a member of the Cumberland Presbyterian Church, and died as she lived, a devoted and consistent Christian.

Five children survive her—Mrs. Helen **Loveland**, living in Ferndale, California; Mrs. Hattie **Biaceo**(?), living in Camden Point; Mrs. Laura **McKinnis**, wife of Prof. W. C.. **McKinnis**, living in Arkansas; William living in Sedalia, and Mollie, wife of Mr. Hayden T. **Leavel**(?) of this county. Of these all were present at her funeral, excepting Mrs. **Loveland** and Mrs. **McKinnis**. The funeral was preached by Rev. D. F. **Bone** and the remains were followed to their last resting place by a large number of old friends and acquaintances.

February 16, 1877

Married

At the residence of the bride's father, William **Morrow**, Esq., by Rev. D. F. **Bone**, Mr. John H. **Stephens** and Miss Ellen S. **Morrow**, all of Clinton County, Mo.

There were perhaps one hundred persons and relations present to do honor to the happy couple. This was one of the most pleasant occasions of the kind ever witnessed by me. We do most heartily wish the parties a long, useful and happy life.
                                                                    D. F. **Bone**

Died—

The many friends of Mr. Jno. **Zarn** will regret to learn of the death of his infant son, Johnny N., which occurred on the 1st inst. The child was aged two months and twenty days.

February 16, 1877 (Continued)

Obituary—

Minnie G. G., daughter of John A. and Sarah E. **Spratt**, died of pneumonia, February 9, 1877, aged 2 years, 5 months and 10 days.

How sad to give up this little lamb, the center of affection in the family circle _?_ below. But the Lord giveth and the Lord taketh away. We have lain her away in the cold ground, but she is not forgotten [Tribute not copied]

Died—

At his residence in Helena, Montana on the 26th of January 1877, Major J. F. **Forbes**, formerly of this county.

The deceased was about 65 years of age. In his younger days he resided in Lincoln County, Kentucky, and was one of the most popular young men in the state. Possessed of a fine person, a gentle disposition, courtly manners and a high sense of honor, he was a welcome visitor at any house, and warmly met by all who knew him. In the social relations, as a husband, a father, a master, he was kind, faithful, affectionate; as a friend, a citizen, a neighbor, he was sincere, hospitable, sympathizing. At a very early period, he embraced Christianity; and here as in other situations, he gave an example most worthy of imitation. He showed himself devoted in heart and meet exemplary the life-always filling his place in the house of God.

Major **Forbes** leaves a large family, a surviving wife, and many dear relations in Kentucky, Missouri and Montana Territory, and a very wide circle of attached friends in mourning and deep distress.

March 2, 1877

Married:

At the residence of the bride's parents in Platte City, by Elder A. F. **Smith**, on Feb 27th, Mr. Sidney **Park** to Miss Hattie **Collins**, daughter of Mr. John **Collins**.

March 2, 1877 (Continued)

In Luck:

Our friend Frank **Williams** came in yesterday and reported a piece of good luck in his family last Tuesday evening. It is of the feminine persuasion and weighed eight pounds. Frank is both proud and happy.

Married: At the residence of the bride's father in Clay County, on the 22nd of Feb. Mr. Robt. **Peters** to Miss Bettie **Williams**. Also at the same time and place, Mr. J. **Moore**, of Clinton County, to Miss America **Williams**, daughters of Mr. Elisha **Williams**.

March 16, 1877

We learn with extreme regret of the death of Mrs. Dora **Rogers**, daughter of Mr. William M. **Couch**, of Platte county. She died in Trinidad, Colorado, where she had gone for the benefit of her health. She was one of the most loveable and accomplished ladies in the west, and her untimely death will be a terrible blow to her parents and friends.

Married:

At the residence of the bride's parents, by Rev. Mr. **Crouch**, on the 14th inst., Mr. David H. **Cole** to Miss Millie **Tinder**, daughter of Mr. Dudley **Tinder**, all of Platte county.

THE LANDMARK most heartily congratulate friend Dave upon the consummation of his fondest hope. He is a big-hearted, generous, and compassionate gentleman, and deserves the great good fortune that has come to him in the shape of as fair and lovely a bride as the sun has ever shone upon.

Died:

On the 8th inst., of consumption, after a protracted illness, at the residence of her brother, S. W. **Herndon**, Mrs. Sue B. **McFarland**, consort of H. **McFarland**, of Plattsburg, Clinton County. The deceased leaves a husband and three children, and a large circle of friends and acquaintenances to mourn her loss. "What God hath given, He hath taken; blessed be his name".

March 16, 1877 (Continued)

Died:

Mrs. Elvira **Guthrie**, wife of Mr. John M. **Guthrie**, died at the family residence in Weston, last Monday. Mrs. **Guthrie** was the daughter of the late Edward **Pence**, one of the earliest settlers of our county, and was a lady of remarkable intelligence and culture. She had been a hopeless invalid for a number of years and had borne her fearful suffering with Christian resignation. The funeral sermon was preached by Elder **Proctor** of the Christian Church, of which she was a zealous member.

March 30, 1877

Mrs. Dora M. Rogers

Mrs. Dora M. **Rogers**, died at Trinidad, Colorado, on Friday, March 9, 1877. Daughter of Wm. And Margaret A. **Couch**, she was born June 5th 1833, in Platte County Mo., where the greater part of her life was spent. A few years during the late war, she lived with her parents in Montana Territory. From 1867-1871, she attended the Christian College at Columbia, Mo, closing her course of study there as a graduate, a cultured and refined lady, and taking with her from the college the hope, esteam, and love of her associates. October 29, 1874, she was married to Dr. **Rogers**, brother of the President of the College she had so long attended, and with him passed the following winter in New York City. With a view of restoring her declining health, in the spring of 1876, she accompanied her husband to Colorado where her death occurred. Her remains were brought back and interred March 14, 1877, in the Parkville cemetery.

Such is the record of some of the more prominent events in the life of a noble and lovely lady. In an uncommon degree, she possessed those highest attributes of womanhood, purity, kindness, charity. With a mind of rare sense, well educated, cultured, and informed from schools, books, travel and a wide rang of experience, she was yet devoid of pretense or affection. Her candor, bearing and prudence inspired confidence and trust. Her fidelity to friends under any and all circumstances, and the high sense of duty and love, with which she discharges all obligations to family and friends, challenged admiration. She was pious in the highest meaning of the word. From such a one, with ample means for the accomplishment of good, the world expected much, and had much need. But too truly has he own favorite exclamation been verified. "How often does the rose of anticipation wither and crumble into the ashes of reality." While still standing in the vestibule of real life, cut down as a flower in full bloom, she is deprived of the fruitation of her opportunities and her toil, only, as we hope, to enjoy them, the more, in the world after life, to which she has gone.

Liberty Advance

March 30, 1877 (Continued)

Married near Barry

March 20th, 1877 by Rev O. D. **Allen**, Mr. W. M. **Endicott**, of Cass County to Miss A. A. **Long**, of Platte County, Mo.

April 6, 1877

A Sad Bereavement-

The family of our estimable fellow citizen, W. G. **Cox** of Green Township has sustained a terrible bereavement in the death of his two children from measles. One of them died on Friday and the other on Saturday, and the two corpses were buried at the same time. Mr. **Cox** was then and is yet seriously ill.

April 27, 1877

Married:

April 12, 1877 at the residence of the bride's father Mr. L. T. **Oliver**, by Rev. D. F. **Bone**, Mr. C. L. **Banning** to Miss Helen M. **Oliver**. There were many friends present to do the happy couple honor and wish them success in life.

Death of an Old Citizen

Mr. David **Nicol**, an old and highly respected citizen, died at his residence about four miles east of Platte City, on Wednesday, April 25th, 1877.

Mr. **Nicol** was born September 17th, 1817, in Rappahannock County, Virginia, and was therefore, at the time of his death, aged fifty-nine years, seven months and eight days. When a young man he married Miss Ellen **Payton**, the faithful and devoted wife who survives him, and in the fall of [1843] he emigrated to Platte county, where he has ever since resided, enjoying to the fullest extent the confidence and esteem of all who knew him.

Birth's, Death's and Marriages from the Platte City Missouri "Landmark"

April 27, 1877 (Continued)

A man of industrious and frugal habits, he accumulated in the course of a busy life a comfortable competence being the owner of one of the best farms in the county. He was singularly quiet and undemonstrative in his disposition, but firm and unalterable in his honest convictions. His was also that type of honesty, characteristic of the hardy pioneers of the Platte Purchase, of whom we say "his word was as good as his bond". He never knowingly wronged any man on earth, and was therefore esteemed a model citizen and a good neighbor.

Mr. **Nicol** leaves a number of children, one of whom is the wife of Mr. Willam A. **Green** of Platte City; another the wife of Dr. B. L. **May**, of Barry, and another the wife of Mr. William **Wood** of St. Louis. The other children are unmarried. The remains of Mr. **Nicol** were borne to the family burying ground of Mrs. M. A. **Marshall** near Platte city yesterday (Thursday) afternoon.

May 4, 1877

--Mr. T. B. **George**, of this county was found standing on his head on Thursday morning, yesterday, Mrs. **George** having jus presented him with a fourteen pound boy. Brack says blood will tell.

Married:

We learn from the St. Joseph *Chronicle* that Mr. Charles W. **Taylor** of Parkville, and Miss Mollie **White**, daughter of Jas. **White**, Esq, of Taos, were married on the 19th of April by Elder J. J. **Wyatt**. We congratulate Charley upon his good fortune, and trust that the skies my never be less bright above him.

Died:

Harry Ross, son of Henry and Myra **Meade**, died last Friday, April 27th, aged eight months and fifteen days. For several days the beautiful little child suffered fearfully from a complication of diseases until death came to his relief. The sympathies of our whole community are enlisted for Mr. and Mrs. **Meade** in their great affliction, for they were devotedly attached to the child, and none but parents who have been similarly bereaved can appreciate their loss.

May 4, 1877 (Continued)

Death of Capt. Wm. H. McPike:

It will no doubt be a painful surprise to the many friends of Capt. William H. **McPike** in this county and elsewhere to hear of his death. For a considerable length of time he had been an invalid suffering with consumption of the bowels, and, in the hope of obtaining relief, he determined to go to Texas, believing that a change of climate would accomplish what medicines had failed to do. He only reached Spring Hill, Johnson County, Kansas, when he could go no further, and there, on Friday, April 27th, at 7 o'clock A.M., he breathed his last. His remains were brought home to Parkville, and on Sunday last the funeral services took place at the M. E. Church, Rev. Mr. **Lewis** officiating, after which a large concourse of people followed his remains to their last resting place in the cemetery. We have not the data at hand to enable us to furnish such a biographical sketch of the deceased as the subject merits. He was born in Buchannan County, Missouri, March 12th, 1838. Of his early life we know comparatively little. At the breaking out of the war he promptly espoused the cause of the South and entered the Confederate army in which he served until the close of the war with distinguished gallantry, rising to the rank of Capitan. His bravery, gallantry, dash, and enterprise as a Confederate soldier made him hosts of friends and crowned him with laurels. He was many times grievously wounded, and more than once left for dead upon the battlefield. It was these old wounds, from which he never fully recovered, that doubtless hastened his death.

He was sober, energetic and enterprising, a firm and unfaltering friend and a magnanimous and generous adversary. A braver or truer man never lived or died, and when Platte County comes to write the history of her gallant sons no name will more deservedly adorn its pages than that of William H. **McPike**.

The deceased was the son-in-law of the late George **Roberts**, of this county, and his wife survives to mourn the loss of a devoted husband.

May 18, 1877

Died:

The wife of Hon. Thos B. **Fenloe** died at Leavenworth last Monday.

Death of Joseph W. Loan:

Last Monday morning, May 14th, at 6'oclock, there died at his residence, two miles east of Platte city, a man in whose life were linked the past and the present and whose history is the history of Platte county. We allude to the death of Joseph W. **Loan**. For several years Mr. **Loan** had been in feeble health which necessarily withdrew him from public life and society, except the companionship of his immediate family and intimate friends. But at last the cycle of his days was complete and he lay down to sleep the sleep of the just. The scriptural allotment of his years was long since complete and death came to him as a blessed relief—his life rounded out with the completeness of duty performed and Christian charity exemplified.

Joseph Wright **Loan** was born in Ligonier Valley Pennsylvania July 28th, 1793. In 1798 with his father's family, he removed to Kentucky, in which state he lived until 1837, when he removed to Missouri. In 1838 he settled in Jackson County, and in March 1841, he removed to Platte County, and settled upon his farm, two miles east of Platte city, where he ever afterwards lived.

He was a soldier of the war of 1812, and served under Col. Richard M. **Johnson** at the battle of the Thomas. He was married in 1818, and of this union nine children were born, of whom six are living: Gen. Benjamin **Loan**, of St. Jo., William, Richard, Charles, Mrs. Mary **Cain**, wife of Wm. **Cain**, of Arago, Nebraska, and Mrs. Bettie **Swain**, wife of John R. **Swain**, of Platte City. All those, we believe were present at the funeral.

Many years ago Mr. **Loan** became a communicant of the M. E. Church, South, and lived and died in the Christian faith, exemplifying in every word and act of his life the sincerity of his profession.

The remains of the deceased were taken to the Methodist Church, last Tuesday, where the funeral services were conducted by Rev. D. F. **Bone**. Afterwards they were conveyed to the **Marshall** burying ground and consigned to mother earth. Among those who stood by the open grave and paid the last tribute of respect to his friend was Uncle Tommy **Jones**, as he is familiarly known, one of the few in Platte county whose age outstripped that of Mr. **Loan**—Mr. **Jones** being upwards of ninety years old.

May 18, 1877 (Continued)

Mr. **Loan** was in every sense of the word a model citizen as well as an exemplary Christian. He was a devoted and affectionate husband and a kind and [____] father. His duty to his neighbor, his State and his country he performed with [____] fidelity. Firm in his own convictions he was tolerant of those of others. Ambitious only to be a good man and true, not a solitary act of selfishness or injustice was ever chargeable against him. He lived revered. He died lamented.

May 25, 1877

Death of Mr. Long:

Died at his residence, in Barry, Platte county, May 11, 1877, with a Christian's hope, Dr. Benj. S. **Long**, aged more than seventy.

He was born Jan. 12th 1808, at Versailles, Woodford county, Ky.—moved with his parents, at an early age to Liberty, Clay county, Mo.—graduated in medicine at the Transylvania Medical College, Lexington, Ky., 1835—was married to Miss Mary **Burnett** in 1836 or 1837, who preceded him to the better land many years. He was again married to Miss Louisa **Basye** in 1848, who also went before in 1864. He leaves one son by the former, and one son and four daughters by the latter marriage to mourn a kind and affectionate father. Realizing that the time of his departure was at hand he bade an affectionate farewell to his children, embraced and kissed the youngest. Then quoting the dying words of T. L. **Parrish**, an old friend, who passed away nearly twenty years ago— "I want to look out upon the world, once more"—he was assisted to the window, and gazing, the last time upon the beautiful green earth, turned to the looking glass and said, "I want to see myself once more," he then walked to the bed, saying as he placed himself thereon, "I am gone" quietly and peacefully fell asleep in death to await the final day when the body shall come forth to eternal life and bloom in its freshness and vigor forever and ever.

He was a faithful member and strong supporter of the Christian Church for 22 years. He was a man of strong mind and general intelligence; a faithful friend, with generous imoulses and one to be missed in society.

The community has lost a good citizen, the medical fraternity a worthy member, the church a faithful brother and strong pillar, the children a warm hearted, kind, loving, and indulgent father and protector, and ourself an intimate friend of thirty years attachment.

Birth's, Death's and Marriages from the Platte City Missouri "Landmark"

May 25, 1877 (Continued)

As a practioner, he was successful, and had few if any superiors. For many years he practiced his profession in Liberty, then Platte City, and finally settled in Barry, where he won the good will, respect and confidence of the people and left us for a better world, without an enemy. May the God he worshipped and served, fulfill the promise " to be a father to the fatherless". A warm attachment of friendship having existed for thirty years between us and the deceased, we offer our condolences to the bereaved children and in silence drop the tear of sympathy over his remains, hoping to strike hands with him on the golden shores beyond the river and join in the glad song of honor, power, glory, and dominion to Him that sits upon the throne.

Clarion

Liberty Tribune

Death of Mrs. Matilda Green:

The sad but not unexpected death of Mrs. Matilda **Green**, wife of Mr. A. N. **Green**, and daughter of Maj. Jesse **Morin**, took place at noon Tuesday, May 22nd. For several months the deceased had been a great sufferer and she only looked forward to the day when death would bring that release which could not be accomplished by human agencies. The deceased was born in Ray County, Missouri January 11th, 1834, and has been a member of the Christian Church ever since she was eighteen years old. In 1854 she was married to Mr. A. N. **Green** and of this union three children survive. In all the varied relations of life, as daughter, wife, a member of the church and of society she performed her duties faithfully and conscientiously and was a good and true woman.

The funeral services were conducted by Elder A. F. **Smith**, at the Christian Church, on Wednesday morning, after which the remains were consigned to their final rest in the **Marshall** burying ground. There has been no death in this community for many years which has aroused so much deep and touching sympathy.

Died:

In Buchanan county on the 19th, inst, of inflammation of the lungs, Katie **Bruce**, daughter of T.P. **Bruce**, Esq., aged 13 years, 5 months and 15 days.

June 15th, 1877

Married:

Elder A. T, **Smith** of this place was married on the 12th inst. to Miss Lizzie **Grimes** of Clay County, Mo.

--Our young, gallant and handsome friend, W.O. **Oldham**, Esq., of this city was presented on Saturday last with eleven pounds of infantile, masculine humanity, being the sixth notch Billy has scored within eleven years, of which four are boys. The *old man* since he has gotten on Church Street, is sanguine his good luck in this respect, promises to be even more flattering than in the past.

Killed By Lightening:

We regret to state that Mr. John **Farra** of the vicinity of New Market, in this county, was struck by lightening on Tuesday evening last, about 7 o'clock, whilst plowing corn, and instantly killed. Mr. **Farra** was about thirty-five years of age and leaves a wife and three children, whom are comfortably provided for. His clothing was entirely burned and torn from his body. The horse he was plowing was knocked down, but recovered. Two men also, about twenty feet from Mr. **Farra**, were knocked down and severely stunned, but since recovered. Mr. **Farra** was a Mason in good standing and one of our best citizens. His remains were buried on Thursday last upon the premises.

June 22, 1877

Death of John Farra

New Market, June 15, 1877—Messrs Editors Landmark—In the last issue of your paper a short notice was given of the death of one of our citizens, John F. **Farra**. Believing that he merits a more extended notice, I address myself to the task.

John F. **Farra** was born in Woodford County, Ky., Oct. 21st, 1845. While quiet young his father came to this state. At an early age John was left an orphan by the death of his father. His mother settled near Platte City, Platte County, and in 1853 removed from thence to this part of the county, and located upon a farm lying one mile west of New Market, upon which the subject of this sketch lived until his death.

His mother married a gentleman by the name of **Fisher**, who survived his marriage only a few years, thus was the family left a second time without a paternal head. The family now consisted of the mother and five boys. In due course of time the two older brothers commenced life's battles for themselves, leaving a large farm together with the care of the family to John, the next oldest boy.

John, though young, soon began to develop those qualities which proclaim the thrifty farmer. He at once set his energies to the task before him and peace and prosperity, like guardian angels, hovered around his home. Not content with becoming a model farmer his untiring zeal still impelled him on until he became one of Platte Countie's first and most successful stock dealers. Though comparatively a young man, his strict integrity and fair dealings left him second to none in his profession. Handling stock was his delight, a ready market was offered the farmers, and we venture the prediction that his place will not easily be supplied.

In the year 1871 he was married to a most worthy young lady, Miss Mary F. **Williams**, (the daughter of one of our oldest citizens, William W. **Williams**) who with three little children, now mourn his loss.

Late Tuesday evening, the 15th inst., while plowing in his field in company with two of his brothers, he was struck by lightening and killed instantly. He was buried with Masonic honors at the family burying ground upon the farm, attended by a large concourse of sorrowing friends. Thus ends the mortal career of one of Platte County's best and most respected citizens.

In the death of John F. **Farra**, this county has lost an enterprising citizen, society a noble ornament, his afflicted family a loving son, husband, father, and brother, and the world an honest man. Peace to his ashes.

W. M. **Middleton**

June 22, 1877 (Continued)

Marriage Bells:

Wedding of Norton B. Anderson, Esq. and Miss Jennie Marshall

One of the brilliant social events that has occurred in this community for many years took place yesterday, June 21st, in the marriage of Norton B. **Anderson**, Esq., and Miss Jennie **Marshall**. It was and event that had long been anticipated and was looked upon as the consummation of a genuine love affair of several years standing. It was definitely announced nearly two weeks ago, and ever since, our local society has been on the *Qui vive* and awaited impatiently the approach of the day.

So yesterday afternoon the Presbyterian Church presented a lively appearance. It was entirely too small for the numbers who desired to be present, but those who gained admission were rewarded with an exhibition of the boasted beauty, wealth, talent, and fashion of our community.

While awaiting the arrival of the wedding party Mrs. **Hawley** performed several overtures upon the organ which were greatly admired. In the meantime Messrs. **Paxton** and **Swain**, as ushers were busily engaged in seating the constantly increasing number of ladies and gentlemen.

Presently the distinguished party arrived, and to the inspiring strains of Straus' Wedding March advanced to the altar, being preceded by Rev. **Penhallegon**, the officiating clergyman. They were arranged about the altar in the following order: Mr. John **Morin** and Miss Phebe **Paxton**, Mr. T. L. **Thomas** and Miss Clemmie **Hatton**, Mr. J. W. **Jenkins** and Miss Maggie **Norton**, and finally the bride and groom. We will not attempt to describe the toilets, as we are not au fait in such things; suffice it to say that on the part of both ladies and gentlemen composing the wedding party the costumes were of the conventional style and fully up to the recognized standard of fashionable attire. The costume of the bride was especially admired, being exquisite in all its details.

When everything was arranged, Rev. **Penhallegon** assumed his station, delivered a brief and appropriate prayer, and proceeded to read the marriage ritual, after which another prayer was made, and, without waiting for the usual congratulations, the party retired, entered carriages and proceeded to the depot, where the bride and groom took the Chicago, Rock Island & Pacific train for Davenport, where they will take a steamer for St. Paul, Minn. Remaining some two weeks.

Thus was consummated one of the pleasantest affairs that ever took place in Platte City, both bride and groom occupying the highest social stations.

June 22, 1877 (Continued)

Mr. **Anderson**, the groom, is a native of Paducah, Ky., and is allied to the first families of the venerable commonwealth. For many years he has been a resident of Platte City, formerly being an associate of Hon. K. H. **Norton** in the practice of law. Judge **Norton** now being on the supreme bench, Mr. **Anderson** has succeeded to his practice, and is accounted one of the foremost young attorneys in Missouri. Besides his fine legal attainments he is among the most through literateures in the state, and was, at one time, associate editor of THE LANDMARK. His bride, Miss Jennie **Marshall**, is the youngest daughter and child of the late Frederick **Marshall**, is finely educated and accomplished and heiress by inheritance of wealth and by divine right of beauty and amiability. It is needless to say that to our young friends not only our congratulations are tendered but also those of all who know them recognize genuine worth and nobleness of character.

May their Northern journey be pleasant, and may they return to us happy and contented, with a future spread out before them bright with the rainbow of promise.

From Parkville:

We had in town last Tuesday morning a very quiet little wedding. Miss Ella, daughter of Dr. J. W. **Ringo**, and M. E. **Thelkeld**, of Jackson County, Mo., were the contracting parties. Prof. **McAfee**, of Park College, was the officiating clergyman. The immediate relatives of the parties were all that were present. We learn that it was a very pleasant affair.

June 29, 1877

Married:

At the residence of the bride's father, Allen **Sloan**, Esq., by Rev. D. F. **Bone**, Mr. John C. **White**, of Leavenworth, Kansas, to Miss Mary F. **Slone**, of Platte County, Mo.

Married:

At the residence of H. F. **Bonner**, at Tracy, near Platte City, by Rev. D. F. **Bone**, on the 27th inst., Hon A. D. **Gilkeson**, of Hays City Kansas, to Mrs. Annie **MacIntosh**, of Leavenworth.

The distinguished bridal party immediately left for the home of the groom at Hayes City. Mr. **Gilkeson** is a member of the Kansas Legislature and at the last session was one of the glorious seventeen Democrats in that Body. He is a fine lawyer and a most companionable gentleman. His bride is a comparative stranger here, but she is handsome and talented. Their new made friends extend to them hearty congratulation.

June 29, 1877 (Continued)

Just His Luck—About the first of the present month our genial friend Frank **Yocum**, clerk of the Weston Court of Common Pleas, became the happy father of a beautiful girl. It makes no difference if he did attempt to palm her off on an innocent community as a boy, it was a girl all the same and Lewis **Siler** will swear to it. Since the date of the happy event we learn that clerk's fees are exacted with the most indiscriminate impartiality and that Frank has eschewed sour mash forever. The last part of this story is apochryphal [sic], as everybody knows.

July 6, 1877

Died:

At the residence of Mr. Eli **Link**, six miles east of Platte City on Saturday, June 30th, George **McAffee**, aged about thirty one years. He was the son of Mr. Geo. **McAffee** the original settler of the quarter section on land upon which Platte City now stands.

July 13, 1877

Death of Noble Richardson

The death of Noble **Richardson** deserves a more extended notice than has been given in the county papers, for he was one of the best and truest citizens of the county, and in his death we have sustained a serious loss.

Noble **Richardson** was born in Kenton County, Ky., in 1826, where he received an excellent education, afterwards graduating in medicine at Cincinnati, but he never practiced his profession to any extent. He removed to Jackson County, Missouri, in 1855. He afterwards removed to Platte County and married Miss. Martha **Wilson**. He was generally engaged in school teaching and farming, being successful in each business. He held the position of Assessor of Carroll Township for several years, the people recognizing his honesty and efficiency by almost unanimously reelecting him. For several years he had been suffering with Consumption and died June 6th, aged fifty years, eight months and six days. He was a moral, upright, conscientious citizen and faithfully performed every duty to society and to his neighbors and his family.

July 27, 1877

Married:

In Monte Lilly's bookstore, in Weston, by Rev. J. W. **Ellis**, on the 20th inst., Mr. John A. **Harvey** and Miss Celia W. **Marshall**, both of Jefferson County, Kansas.

In Weston, on the 19th inst, by Judge W. H. **Roney**, at the residence of Mr. Joel **Simmons**, Mr. Hartman **Schneider** and Miss Mary **Simmons**.

Married:

On Wednesday evening last, by the Rev. J. B. **McCleary**, of Leavenworth, at the residence of the bride's parents, Mr. Stephen **Johnson**, of Platte City, to Miss Ida **Clay**, daughter of Thomas **Clay**, Esq., of Clinton county, Mo.

The attendants were Messrs. George **Mason** and T. L. **Thomas** and Misses Jennie **Clemmings** and Clemmie **Hatton**.

Quite a number of ladies and gentlemen were in attendance from Leavenworth and Platte City, besides a large number of friends from Clinton and Platte counties.

The happy couple will make their future residence in Platte City.

We wish them a long life of prosperity and unadulterated happiness.

August 3, 1877

Col. A. G. Blakey

The telegraph brings the melancholy news of the death of Col. A. G. **Blakey**, proprietor of the Pleasant Hill *Review,* a Pleasant Hill, last Saturday, July 28th…

Birth's, Death's and Marriages from the Platte City Missouri "Landmark"

August 3, 1877 (Continued)

Death of an Old Citizen:

Robert C. **Ellifrit**, one of the oldest and most prominent citizens of Weston, died in that City July 31st, aged seventy years. He was born in Virginia, and at an early day emigrated to Missouri. He was a large hearted, intelligent and public-spirited man, and before old age rendered it impractible, was deeply interested in all measures looking to the advancement of his county and State. He was an earnest member of the Presbyterian Church and his daily walk and conversation were consistent with his profession. He was a kind husband and father and an upright, honorable citizen. He was the father of our townman, Mr. R. T. **Ellifrit**, the druggist.

Fatal Accident:

On Thursday of last week Mr. James **Helvey**, an old and prominent citizen of Weston, was run over by a wagon loaded with wood, and sustained injuries from which he died in a few hours.

Sudden Death—

Mrs. Samuel **Call**, and old and respected lady of this county, went to DeKalb last Saturday, and returning, just as she reached the door of her residence, dropped dead. Mrs. **Call** was a very old lady and was related to the best families in Northwest Missouri.

Wooden Wedding:

Last Tuesday evening, Mr. and Mrs. W. R. **Wills** celebrated their wooden wedding. At an early hour a large number of friends began to assemble at their residence, each bearing with him or her some wooden present, as their fancy suggested, many of them useful, and others to afford amusement. After all had arrived, filling the house to its fullest capacity, the bride and groom of five years presented themselves, and Rev. Henry **Meades** made a brief address and caused them to renew their vows. It was a very pleasant episode and Mr. **Meads** did himself great credit by the inimitable style in which he performed his duties. After the ceremony the company was invited to participate in a repast such as seldom been spread in Platte City. Everything that the market could afford or the culinary taste devise was in lavish abundance.

We congratulate Mr. and Mrs. **Wills** upon their five years of happiness and prosperity and wish an equal good fortune will attend them through all their future.

Birth's, Death's and Marriages from the Platte City Missouri "Landmark"

August 3, 1877 (Continued)

The following is a partial list of presents and donors;

Pie lifter, Miss Jane **Coleman**; Foot tub, Jas. **Flannery**; Butter mould, Mrs. T. H. **Coleman**; Work basket, Dr. and Mrs. **Coffey**; Bucket, Miss Cassie **Coleman**; Fancy thread box, Chas. B. **Kurtz**; Potato masher, Mrs. A. J. **Coleman**; Knife basket, Mrs. Billy **Oldham**; Sugar box, Geo. **Cartwright**; Wooden shoes, John **Zarn**; Duster, Nealy **Lutes**; Corner bracket, Willie **Guthrie**; Portable hat rack, Mr. and Mrs. C. B. **Hawley**; Butter mould, H. C. **Coleman**; Water Bucket, Mrs. John **Brady**; Butter paddle, Mrs. **Hollingsworth**; Clothes pins, A. J. **Coleman**; Wooden ink stand, S. D. **Brady**; Chromo, Miss. Emma **Boyd**; Clothes pins, Arthur G. **Meade**; Mouse trap, Percy **Hawley**; Water bucket, Clint **Cockrill**; Cane, Mr. Billy **Oldham**; Market basket, T. W. **Park**; Stick of wood, F. M. **Green** & Co.; Match, Willie **Boyd**: Checker board, Mrs. Henry **Meade**.

There were other presents not bearing cards.

Died:

At Daughters' College, near Platte City, Mo., on Friday morning July 27, 1877, Zon, infant daughter of T. W. and Maggie E. **Park**, aged one month.

Died:

At his residence in Platte county, Mo., July 19, 1899, Charles **Stout**, only son of Mr. and Mrs. **Stout**, aged 27 years, 7 months, and 3 days.

His health had been declining for several years, yet he was of an active, energetic disposition, always alive to business. He was an affectionate husband, good citizen and kind neighbor.

Although he had been baptized and had been a member of the Reformed Church, he never felt just ready to enter on the future state till but just shortly before his death. His last illness was protracted and his sufferings were unremitting and sometimes extreme; but the grace of God was sufficient for him. When he became aware that his sickness might and certainly would be unto death, he commenced setting his house in order. I was permitted to be with him a great deal during his sickness, and often heard him speak in rapture of his bright prospects of again meeting his dear children, (over the river) one of whom had preceded him but a few days. He called his friends to his bedside and asked God to bless them and exhorted them to live right and meet him in heaven. His last moments were calm and peaceful. He leaves a young wife (the only daughter of J. H. and E. **Maupin**,) kind parents and an aged grandmother to mourn his loss. His funeral was well attended. Many relatives, friends and neighbors followed his remains to their last resting place there to await the resurrection morn. The righteous hath hope in his death.

August 10, 1877

Died:

In Elk County, Kansas, on Sunday July 22nd, with congestive chill, Robert Edgar, oldest son of Henry and Charity **Cooper**. Little Robert was born in Platte County, Mo., August 14th, 1870. He was at the time of his death 6 years, 11 months, and 8 days old.

August 17, 1877

Funeral:

The funeral of Mrs. Lucinda **Fox**, mother of Mr. Wm. A. **Fox**, will be preached by the Rev. C. I. **Vandeventer** at Hickory Grove Church, on the first Sunday in September.

Death of W. G. Cox:

Mr. W. G. **Cox**, one of the wealthiest and most influential farmers in Platte County, died at his residence near New Market, on the 11 inst., aged about fifty-five years. For many months he has been seriously ill and his death was not unexpected. Mr. **Cox** was born in Scott County, Kentucky, and removed to Platte County in 1853. During his residence her he accumulated a handsome fortune. He was a prudent and very successful farmer and trader, and his farm is considered one of the best in the county. He was one of the most generous and hospitable of men, and his home was a favorite place of resort for young and old. Platte County never boasted a better citizen or a more upright man. He leaves a wife and several children.

August 24, 1877

Married:

At the residence of Mrs. **Bailey**, in Platte County, Mo., August 14, 1877 by Rev. W. S. **Connor**, Mr. J. J. **Baker** of Doniphan county, Kansas, to Miss. Julia **Andrews** of Platte county, Mo.

September 7, 1877

Married:

At the residence of the bride's parents, near New Market, in this county, September 5th, by Elder W. C. **Rogers**, Mr. Eli **Owens** to Miss Mary **Middleton**, daughter of Mr. Robt. M. **Middleton**, all of this county.

Married:

Last Thursday, August 30th, the neighborhood of Smithville witnessed the nuptials of two of the best known of the young folk of the vicinity. At that time, at the residence of the bride's father, Mr. **John Thatcher**, Elder B. **Waller** united in marriage Mr. Edgar **Spratt** and Miss. Sibbie **Thatcher**. The attendants were Mr. Jake **Link** and Miss Bettie **Berryman**.

The groom is one of the most courteous and intelligent young men of the county, while the bride is noted for her beauty, intelligence and amiability. THE LANDMARK wishes them a long life of happiness and prosperity.

Died:

August 31, 1877, Mary E., infant daughter of R. J. and H. J. **Mayo**, aged 4 months and 18 days.

The mother and six children are gone home to God, and the father and six children still linger on the shores of time. Indeed, this is a "vale of tears" to Bro. **Mayo**. May the great Shepherd and Bishop of Souls take care of the father and the dear little children who yet remain among us, and bring them all to a happy reunion in the Heaven of their hopes.

D. F. Bone

Death of Fred Hoeck:

On Thursday of last week Mr. Fred **Hoeck** died at his residence in Weston, aged fifty-three years. He leaves a wife and seven children. He was buried by the Odd-Fellows and the German Benevolent Society of Weston, of which orders he was an exemplary and zealous member. Mr. **Hoeck** s a German by birth, but had lived in Weston for more than twenty years, and for many years had been connected with the brass bands there. Has was a warm hearted generous man, full of kind impulses and ready at all times to administer to the wants of the distressed or to assist a friend. He leaves many friends behind to mourn his loss.

September 21, 1877

Married:

At the residence of the bride's parents, near Platte City, by Elder A. F. **Smith**, on the 13th inst., Mr. Benjamin **Montague** to Miss Bettie **Murdock**, all of Platte county.

Married:

At Smith's Ferry, near Farley, by Esquire **Spratt**, on the 13th inst., Mr. James **Bryant** to Mrs. Mattie **Ford**, all of Platte County.

Married:

Hon. E. H. **Norton**, of the Supreme Court of Missouri, and Mrs. M. A. **Marshall** were married at the residence of the latter last Monday, Sept. 17th, Rev. W. H. **Penhallegon** officiating. Only a few relatives and intimate friends were present, and immediately the distinguished groom and bride took the train for New York and a tour through the Eastern States. Their many friends wish them a pleasant trip and long lives of honor and happiness.

September 28, 1877

Died of Consumption:

New Market, Sept. 22, 1877. On the 2nd day of the present month, Mrs. Paula **Armstrong**'s spirit passed to other spheres.

Mrs. **Armstrong**, daughter of Henry and Elizabeth **Harlan**, was born in Boyle county, Kentucky, on the 7th day of Sept., 1840. She emigrated to this State in the spring of 1856, and in October 1857, was married to Harlan **Baughman**. When the shot that crashed through Sumptner's walls, told of oppression and war, Mr. **Baughman**, like hundreds of others, he left his home never more to return. Some time after the death of Mr. **Boughman** Mrs. **Boughman** was married to C. P. **Armstrong**, a prominent citizen and businessman of this place, where with the exception of a few months, she lived until her death.

Birth's, Death's and Marriages from the Platte City Missouri "Landmark"

September 28, 1877 (Continued)

Mrs. **Armstrong** was never robust. Her form was cast in delicate mould, her nervous organization was highly strung; yet she possessed a wiry toughness of muscular fever and an impending will which succumbed, but slowly, to the disease that preyed upon her. The battle was fought long and well, but the grim monarch finally planted his flag upon the citadel of life.

Mrs. **Armstrong** had a warm heart, and while she felt keenly any injustice done her, she loved her friends with the whole fervor of her impulsive nature. When trusted friends were wanted to keep their nightly vigil around the bedside of the sick and suffering, Mrs. **Armstrong** stood foremost. A call of sorrow or want awakened every fiber of her sympathetic soul, and no call of charity ever came to her door unheeded. Hers was the smile of welcome, hers the tear of sympathy; but the time came when instead of giving, she needed all those friendly offerings. For years she lay upon the bed of affliction, her poor body racked and tortured by disease, yet, with the Christian's hope to bear her on and upward, she met death calmly, expressing herself that she was not afraid to die.

Our sister has gone, yet may we rest in the hope that she has left all these sorrows behind her, and that she has gone to that land where pain and sickness never come.

We tender our Christian sympathies to her bereaved family, hoping the separation may not be final, and that her husband and daughter may so conduct themselves through life, that there may be a grand reunion beyond the shores of time.

W. **Middleton**

Birth:

It was a girl this time at Tom **Jenkins**', and Tom declares she is the handsomest young lady in this State.

Death:

Peter **Blancjour**, a well known citizen of Weston, died on Tuesday morning, aged about sixty-seven years. For many years and until recently he was Postmaster at Weston.

--Mr. Neal **Lutes** has been setting 'em up to the boys this week, all because he has had an addition to his family in the person of a boy whose avoirdupois is boldly asserted to be thirteen pounds.

September 28, 1877 (Continued)

Married:

Last Sunday, after considerable delay and embarrassment, Mr. Thomas **Patton** of Leavenworth, and Miss. Mollie **Berry**, of Wyandotte county, Kansas, were married by Esq. Probasco **Thomas** at his residence. The eloping couple were accompanied by Mr. Dock **Mattox** and Miss. Mollie **Patton**, and Mr. James A. **King** and Miss Sadie **Patton**.

Married:

Morgan-Cain. In the Christian Church, at College city, Cal., on Wednesday evening, Sept. 19th, 1877, by Eld J. C. **Keith**, Mr. L. M. **Morgan** and Miss Sue E. **Cain**, both formerly of Missouri.

October 12, 1877

Died:

Mr. Thomas J. **Brasfield**, for many years an old and respected citizen of Platte and Clay counties, died at Harlem last Tuesday, aged seventy-three years. He was a native of Clark County, Kentucky, and a relative of Judge John S. **Brasfield** of this county, at whose burying ground the remains were buried last Wednesday.

Birth:

We are informed that the estimable wife of Mr. Wm. **Fleshman** (Buck) was presented on Tuesday morning last with a thirteen pounder, who has since been named after his illustrious grandsire, Justice Washington **Mayo**. The boy is one of the largest that has ever made his debut in the county. We understand that "Buck" is doing as well as could be expected under all the circumstances.

October 12, 1877 (Continued)

Married:

In THE LANDMARK office, Platte City, Mo., by Esquire G. W. **Mayo**, on Thursday, October 11th, 1877, Mr. Francis A. **Feeback** and Mrs. Jane **Racey**, both of Platte county, Mo.

The interesting ceremony was performed in the presence of Miss Mamie **Burnes** and Messrs. W. P. **White**, J. J. **Park**, J. H. **Chinn**, R. T. **Darnall**, J. T. **Reynolds**, THE LANDMARK staff and others. May prosperity ever attend the happy couple.

Married:

On Tuesday evening at the residence of the bride's father, one mile north of Platte City, by the Rev. W. A. **Crouch**, Mr. John T. **Hayes**, of Mansfield, Illinois, to Miss Mary C. daughter of David S. **Fisher**, of Platte county.

A large number of friends and acquaintances were present at the ceremony and did ample justice to the bountiful collation spread in honor of the occasion. On Wednesday afternoon the happy pair took their departure for their future home in Illinois, bringing with them the heartfelt wishes of all for their future prosperity and happiness, to which THE LANDMARK adds its greetings.

Resolutions of Respect:

From the Church of Christ meeting in New Market, Mo. For the death of John B. **Dean**...

[Date of death not stated]

October 19, 1877

Marriage of Mr. T. L. Thomas and Miss LeVerrier Johnson

Social circica in Platte City have been of the *qui vive* for some time on account of the approaching nuptials of Mr. T. L. **Thomas**, teller of the Farmers' National Bank, and Miss LeVerrier **Johnson**. This event took place on the evening of Thursday, October 18th, 1877, Elder A. F. **Smith** officiating. It was strictly a private and quiet affair, no cards being issued and nobody present except the relatives and a few intimate friends.

The groom is one of the best young businessmen of the city, of pleasing address, and excellent moral character.

The bride is one of the most beautiful and charming young ladies in the community and has long been the pride of our best social circles. Her beauty is of that type that arrests every eye, while her grace is something to dream and remember. Combined with these she possesses all those amiable qualities which make her loved and loveable and so well adapt her to adorn domestic as well as social life.

This being a true love match, we may confidently anticipate for our young friends a wedded life full of bliss.

In all their future the good wishes of none flow out more fully to Tup. And LeVerrier than from THE LANDMARK, and we cast after them with hearty good will our "old shoe"

Marriage Bells:

One of the most interesting social events that has occurred in the lower part of the county, took place at the residence of Capt. Thomas **Henry**, near Prairie Point, on Thursday, September 10. 1877. It was the wedding of Mr. Levi A. **Link** and Miss Frankie **Henry**, both of this county. The interesting ceremony was performed by Rev. Father **Handley**, of Liberty, in the presence of a large number of the neighbors and intimate friends of the young couple who extended most hearty congratulations. The repast that was spread by the parents of the bride in honor of the event was most sumptuous and comparted with their well known hospitality and generous manner of dispensing it.

The next evening there was a most elegant reception given the wedded pair at Mr. Eli **Link**'s, the grooms father, where about one hundred guests had gathered to do their honor. It was a delightful affair and will long be a pleasant memory.

The groom is one of the most successful young farmers and traders in the county and is noted for his affability and kind curious being.

October 19, 1877 (Continued)

The bride, the daughter of Capt. Thos. **Henry**, one of our leading agriculturists and most popular citizens, is a charming beauty, unsurpassing grace and superior accomplishments.

THE LANDMARK tenders its warmest congratulations.

Double Wedding:

Last Monday in Green township, Mr. L.L. **Lamar** and Miss Carrie **Beck**, Mr. F. **Lamar** and Miss Lou **Beck**, were married by Rev. J. **Clay**. The Messers. Lamar are brothers and are noted as being the most industrious and thrifty of our young farmers. We congratulate the happy couples and wish them a long life and joy in their new relation.
Weston Commercial

November 2, 1877

Died:

Mrs. Isabella **Stallard**, wife of Mr. Marcellus **Stallard**, of Camden Point, died of consumption at the residence of her father, Mr. Ran. **Duncan**, October 25th, aged about twenty-three years. Mrs. **Stallard** had only been married a few months, and her untimely death must be a terrible bereavement for her husband and for all those to whom she had endeared herself by her kindness and affection.

November 9, 1877

Married:

It is strange that it did not come to our knowledge sooner, but it did not, we mean the marriage of Mr. George **Ireland** to Miss Annie **Winn**. The ceremony was performed by Elder A. F. **Smith**, on the 10th of October, at the residence of James E. **Ireland**, of Lee Township. Though late in making the announcement, we hope we are not too late to extend a hearty congratulations to our young friends and to chide them for keeping the affair so quiet.

November 23, 1877

Died:

On the 19th inst., of consumption, Robert **Denton**, at his brother's residence, six miles south of Platte City, aged about twenty-eight years.

On the 18th inst., Kendrick **Waller** of this county, at the residence of his mother, aged about twenty-two years.

Married:

On the 21st inst., by Elder A. F. **Smith**, Mr. John Churchwill **Walker**, to Miss Emma **Banning**, all of Platte County.

On the 20th inst., by Rev. B. **Waller**, Mr. P. W. **Chinn**, to Miss Fannie **Dougherty**, all of Platte county. We bespeak for the happy couple a long life of happiness, and a full compliment of **Chinn** music to keep all aware that the *pater familias* is ever alert.

November 30, 1877

Married:

Mr. Joseph **Thatcher** and Miss. Tinnie **Hall** were married on the 15th inst., near [Go_neyville]. We wonder of this is our Joe.

November 30, 1877 (Continued)

SURRENDERED—

It was not "Chief Joseph" nor "Sitting Bull" this time, but no less a personage than Clark **Brown**, Esq., of this county, surrendering himself to the charms of a handsome young lady. For some time past Clark had been very reticent and non communicative, and the sequel to his conduct is described in these hues:

>"He had cast no missile
>At the social law's epistle
>Nor had ever harmed a dove
>He was simply in the _____
>And the sleep defying stillness
>Of a trying case of love"

The happy bride was Miss Susan **Gibson**, daughter of Hon. John **Gibson**, of Ontario, Canada. The marriage occurred in Leavenworth, Kansas, on the 15th inst. The romantic part of the affair is that Clark had never seen the lady until about two hours previous to the ceremony, epistolary correspondence being the means which he used in winning his fair bride, another instance showing the "might of the pen". The bride and groom have our congratulations.

Died:

At his residence in Lee Township, of paralysis, on the 26th inst., Mr. James **White**, aged about fifty-five years.

In Farley on the 25th inst., an infant child of Mr. Geo. **Canby**.

In this place, at the residence of her parents on the 24th inst., of consumption, Mrs. Mary L., wife of James F. **Flannery**. Mrs. **Flannery** was born in Platte County, Missouri, July the 17th, 1849, and was married February the 8th, 1871. She became a member of the M.E. Church South in the fall of 1866. She was a most devoted wife and one of the very best women the community could boast of. She leaves a stricken husband and two sorrowing little girls to mourn their sad loss, and who have the sympathies of our entire population in this sad hour of their affliction.

The Rev. Mr. **Campbell** officiated at the funeral and the remains were borne to our city cemetery, followed by a large concourse of relatives and deeply afflicted friends.

November 30, 1877 (Continued)

Death of Nicholas Timberlake:

Died at his residence in Farley, Nov. 25th, 1877, Nicholas **Timberlake**, aged forty-seven years and nineteen days.

The deceased was a Kentuckian by birth, but early emigrated to this county with his father, John **Timberlake**.

He married early and commenced merchandising in Parkville. Failing in business there, he gave up the life of a merchant and moved on the farm now occupied by John **Brannan**, five miles east of Farley. From there he moved to Farley and was engaged in various pursuits until his death. He has been a man unusually healthy and until his last fatal sickness had seldom been unwell. He was taken the first of last week with pneumonia, and called in Dr. J. M. **Holt**, who attended him until his death. But death had marked him for his own and human aid was powerless.

He died beloved and lamented by his family and friends, and respected by all who knew him. His remains were interred at the Green graveyard on Tuesday, November 27th.

December 7, 1877

Died:

The venerable Mrs. **Hon**, wife of Mr. Issac **Hon**, of this county, died last Sunday at a very advanced age.

Died:

Mr. Archibald **Wills**, of this county, died last Monday night, aged eighty seven. He was a soldier of the war of 1812 and settled in Platte County in 1837, where he has ever since lived respected and beloved.

Death of Mrs. Clemmie Field:

The death of this lovely women has thrown a cloud over the whole community. Her protracted illness, and her complicated disease, have, for months, called for sympathy and assistance. A mother's affectionate care has been lavished on her first-born; a sister's

December 7, 1877 (Continued)

voice has tenderly consoled the suffering one; and loving companions have strewn roses around her couch.

Mrs. **Field** was the oldest child of the late Dr. Frederick **Marshall**. She was born November 16, 1844; was married to William H. **Field**, on her twenty-first birthday, and died Dec. 3d, 1877. Her mother—now the wife of Hon. E. H. **Norton**, judge of the Supreme Court of the State—survives her; and three little children—Julia, Jennie and Marshall weep with those around them, though they are scarcely conscious of their irreparable loss.

When quite young Mrs. **Field**—then Clemmie **Marshall**—united with the Presbyterian church of Platte City, under the care of Rev. J. G. **Fackler**. She continued a member until her death, taking a lively interest in every good cause. Her talent for music won her many [?]. In the Sabbath School she led the choir, and in every entertainment she was a welcome guest. Her accomplishments and her affectionate heart made her the center of a large circle of worthy companions.

A few hours before her death, as the Sabbath sun made bright the closing day, I visited her couch of suffering, in company with an intelligent minister. She at once asked him to speak to her of heaven. He accordingly read to her of the delights of the upper world. He then, with the weeping family and friends, knelt in fervent prayer for the dying Christian. Mrs. **Field** then had her three children brought to her couch, and, in a second prayer, they were committed to the keeping of their Father in heaven. 'Twas a lovely sight when little Marshall knelt down so sweetly by his dying mother while the man of God, with one hand on the child's head, and the other pointed to heaven, asked a blessing for the weeping children.

During the early part of the night that followed these affecting ceremonies, Mrs. **Field** appeared to be communing with the Savior she loved. After midnight an attendant observed her countenance wreathed in smiles, and her eyes fixed intently on heaven. She inquired: "Clemmie, my dear, what do you see?" The dying women answered, "Angels, Oh, so many and so beautiful!" A half hour later she said, "The Angels, the beautiful angels!" In a short time she calmly and sweetly expired, with the smile of ineffable peace still resting on her features.

[Tribute entitled "Angels" not copied here]

Married:

Mr. R. Bunyan **Smith** and Miss Martha E. **Spicer** were married November 23rd, 1877 by Rev. O. D. **Allen**, at the residence of the bride's father.

December 7, 1877 (Continued)

Mr. **Smith** is a sterling young man and his bride is the amiable daughter of Hiram **Spicer**, Esq., one of our oldest and most esteemed citizens, living on the east side of the county.

Death of an Estimable Lady:

Last Tuesday we received the sad news of the death of Mrs. Sarah **Thatcher**, wife of John **Thatcher**, of Smithville, and daughter of Mr. William S. **Kerr**, of this county. It occurred at Pueblo, Colorado, last Saturday, whither she had gone in the vain hope of securing relief from that dreadful malady, consumption. Her remains were brought to Platte County and [__?__] to their final resting place in the family burying ground. Mrs. **Thatcher** was one of the loveliest and most amiable ladies of the county and her untimely death will bring sorrow to many a heart.

Death of Mrs. Clemmie Field:

Mrs. Clemmie **Field** died at the residence of Norton B. **Anderson**, Esq., in Platte City, last Monday morning at 3 o'clock, after a long illness, of consumption. It is true that for several weeks her death had been expected, and the minds of her friends were as fully prepared for the melancholy event as the warnings of disease could make them; but it is simple truth to day that no death in our community has brought with is more universal and heartfelt regret than that of Mrs. **Field**.

The deceased was the eldest daughter of the late Dr. Frederick **Marshall**, and was born November 16th, 1841, in Platte City, where she has ever since resided. Her education was obtained in the schools of Platte City and Liberty. On the twenty-first anniversary of her birth she was married to Mr. Wm. H. **Field**, and of this union her three children, Julia, Jennie and Marshall, survive her. In 1861 she became a member of the Presbyterian Church and lived and died in that faith, an earnest, consistent and devoted member.

For years she had been suffering from consumption and realized fully that her days on earth were but few. The close of her life was calm peaceful and beautiful. Kind hands administered to her every want, and tenderest affection hovered constantly about her bedside. About sunset of her last evening, looking through the open doorway, for the last time, she said, "the sky never seemed so blue and beautiful before", and a few hours before her death, when Nature's machinery was nearly run down, illumined by the supreme faith within her soul, she said, "Oh"! The beautiful angels! They are hovering about me" and asked those around her if they, too, could not see them. And making her dying bequests, tenderly committing her little children to those whose greatest pleasure it will be to protect them in the future, and bidding a final farewell to all, she sank into that dreamless slumber that comes at last to all humanity.

December 7, 1877 (Continued)

The funeral services took place on Tuesday afternoon at the Presbyterian Church and were conducted by Rev. W. H. **Penhallegon**, assisted by the Rev. Mr. **Campbell**. Mrs. **Field** had formerly, until stricken by disease, been the leader of the church choir and during the funeral exercises the remaining members of the choir sang a number of beautiful songs, favorites of the deceased. Rev. Mr. **Penhallegon's** allusions to the life and death of Mrs. **Field**, were beautifully appropriate. At the conclusion of the exercises the coffin was uncovered and the large audience of friends took a final look at her face, after which the body was conveyed to the family burying ground, and by tender hands lowered to its chosen resting place at the feet of her deceased father.

Happiness does not always come to those most deserving it, and surely her feet trod the wine-press of life and her lips drank deeply of its bitter [?]. But from life's pains and misfortunes was developed a character of singular loyal ness, and about which was gathered a friendship that was devotion.

Tender hearted and charitable, she was a ministering angel in the midst of suffering and affliction. The poor felt the touch of her gentle hand, and the sick found her sleepless at her bedside.

It seems strange and hard that one so young, so beautiful, with so much to live for, so tender and loving in all the relations of life, should be taken away, but if ours it is to quaff the cup of sorrow, may we hope it is her's to win thee crown of life in the blessed [?].

December 14, 1877

Died:

Mr. Isaac N. **Moody** died of typhoid fever at the residence of his father-in-law, M. David **Newman**, in Preston Township, last Tuesday, aged twenty-eight. He leaves a wife and two children. He was buried by the Masonic brotherhood of Union Mills on Wednesday. Mr. **Moody** was a moral and upright man and an excellent citizen.

Married:

Mr. D. J. **Link** and Mrs. Emma **Richardson** were married by Elder B. **Waller**, at the residence of the bride, on Tuesday, the 11th inst. From all accounts there was a royal feast and a jolly good party to do justice to it and to give the wedded pair a good send-off.

December 14, 1877 (Continued)

In the evening the party repaired to the residence of the groom and there another feast awaited them, after which a glorious old-fashioned dance was indulged in.

Mr. **Link** is one of our best and most prosperous farmers, while his bride, the sister of W. J. and J. C. **Summers** and Mrs. Fielding **Burnes**, is one of the best and most amiable ladies in the county. THE LANDMARK extends its heartiest congratulations.

December 21, 1877

Died:

In Platte City, Dec. 14th, Erle **Marshall**, infant son of the late A. G. **Marshall** and Mrs. Mary E. **Marshall**, aged thirteen months.

Died:

Friday, the 11th inst., Geo S. **Breckenridge**, age 13 years, five months and seven days. The deceased was a grand son of Mr. Elmore **Breckenridge**, one of the oldest settlers in Platte and a lineal descendant of the **Breckenridge** family of Kentucky. Being in robust health and of a strong constitution the family had not dreamed of his death until sometime in the day preceding it, when he was taken with a violent attack of the measles. Thus another bright and interesting boy has been snatched from the bosom of relatives and friends and the neighborhood received a warning that death is no respecter of age. The relatives and friends have the sympathy of the entire community in this their sad bereavement.

Died:

In Napa Valley, Cal., November 23, Garrard **Long**, aged 68, and for over 10 years a resident of Clay.

Married:

At the residence of Dr. E. McD. **Coffey**, in Platte City, by Elder A. F. **Smith**, on the 17th inst., Mr. John **Mason**, of Ray county, Mo., and Mrs. L. S. **Williams**, sister of Dr. E. McD. **Coffey**. The affair was strictly private, and the groom and bride immediately left for their future home. The bride is well known to all our citizens and they all will heartily unite with us in tendering our congratulations.

Birth's, Death's and Marriages from the Platte City Missouri "Landmark"

December 21, 1877 (Continued)

Married:

On the 12th inst., at the residence of Mr. F. M. **McVey**, by Eld A. **Proctor**, Mr. John D. **Robinson** and Miss Mollie E., daughter of Mrs. Mary E. **Oldham**, of Platte county, Mo.

Married:

At the residence of Mr. William **Daniels**, by Eld. A. F. **Smith**, on the 18th inst., Mr. Hiram **McComas** and Miss Mammie **Daniels**, all of this county.

Married:

On Tuesday, Dec. 18th at the residence of the bride's parents, Mr. Luther **Stallard**, of Kansas, and Miss Lizzie **Humphrey**, of this county.

Quite a goodly number of friends assembled on the occasion to witness the nuptial ceremonies and tender their congratulations. The bride is one of the best and loveliest of Platte's fair daughters, and the groom, also a Platte countian, is everything that is true hearted and noble in man. He has a bride equal to his desserts and we sincerely congratulate him. For their kindly remembrance of THE LANDMARK we especially thank all parties.

Married:

On the 20th inst., by Rev. W. C. **Campbell**, Mr. Larkin E. **Tinder** to Miss Charlotte **Jones**, all of this county.

Birth's, Death's and Marriages from the Platte City Missouri "Landmark"

Name Index

Name	Page
Adams, Martha Elizabeth	3
Adams, Smith	3
Adkins, Anna	4
Adkins, Bluford	4
Adkins, Della M.	28
Adkins, Granville	28
Adkins, Granville (Mrs.)	28
Aker, P. (Elder)	79
Aker, Preston	76
Aker, Sallie	76
Akers, Joseph	17
Akers, Sallie	74
Alexander, John	78
Alexander, Luella	52
Algier, James	45
Allen, F. W. (Elder)	44
Allen, O. D. (Rev.)	88, 113
Allen, Wm.	11
Allin, Dulcy D.	55
Allin, Major	55
Almond, Clara	62
Almond, W. B.	62
Alvis, Thomas	14
Anderson, Mr. John	65
Anderson, Nannie	6
Anderson, Norton B.	96, 114
Andrews, Julia	102
Armstrong, (Mr.)	33
Armstrong, Belle	47
Armstrong, C. P. (Hon.)	47
Armstrong, C. P. (Mrs.)	33
Armstrong, C.P.	104
Armstrong, Mr. William H.	62
Armstrong, Paula	104
Arnold, Mary	81
Ashby, Lizzie J.	1
Avery, Mr. (Rev.)	19
Babcock, Mr.	49
Baber, Delilah	72
Bailey, Granville G.	2
Bailey, Mr.	36
Bailey, Mrs.	102
Baker, C. T.	33
Baker, Henry	33
Baker, J. H.	33
Baker, J. J.	102
Baker, Mrs.	57
Baker, W. H. H.	52
Ballard, W. H.	65
Bane, Louisa	77
Banning, C. L.	46, 88
Banning, Cole L	6
Banning, Emma	110
Banning, Esquire	53
Banning, George H.	6
Banning, Huldah	6
Basye, Arlie	50
Basye, Henry	50
Basye, Louisa	92
Baughman. Harlan	104
Baughmann, T. M.	81
Beagle, J. A. (Rev.)	65
Beagle, John A. (Rev.)	60
Beck, Carrie	109
Beck, Lou	109
Becker, Julius	45
Beery, Bell	10
Beery, Esq.	9
Beery, J. (Esq.)	2
Beery, Jeramiah	12
Beery, John A.	10
Beery, Widow	67
Belt, George W.	41
Belt, Lizzie	41
Berger, Julius	64
Berry, Jeremiah (Esquire)	9
Berry, Mollie	106
Berryman, Bettie	43, 103
Betts, Mr. (Rev.)	28
Biaceo, Hattie	84
Bigham, John	75
Bixey, W. W.	83
Black, William	10
Blakely, Jesse	52
Blakely, John C.	52
Blakey, A. G.	99
Blakey, J. Y. (Rev.)	1
Blakley, Felix	52

Birth's, Death's and Marriages from the Platte City Missouri "Landmark"

Name	Page
Blakley, Proman	1
Blancjour, Peter	105
Blanton, Sheba	30
Bledsoe, Willis (Dr.)	73
Blesdoe, Mildred	39
Bone, D. F.	61, 78
Bone, D. F. (Rev.)	45, 52, 53, 62, 67, 69, 70, 77, 78, 81, 84, 88, 91, 97
Bonnel, W. D.	11
Bonner, H. F.	97
Borden, Dan	52
Boyd, Emma	101
Boyd, Isreal	2
Boyd, Willie	101
Bradley, Florence	9
Bradley, J. P.	2
Bradley, Jackson	9
Bradley, Mary	39
Brady, John (Mrs.)	101
Brady, Mary E.	14
Brady, S. D.	101
Brannan, John	112
Brasfield, T. W. R.	64
Brasfield, John S.	64, 106
Brasfield, Thomas J.	106
Brasfield, Ellen	64
Brasficld's, Judge	24
Breckenridge, Elmore	116
Breckenridge, Fanute	3
Breckenridge, Geo. S.	116
Brill, Edward	48
Broadhurst, C. W.	51
Brock, Wm A.	78
Bronaugh, Anna	80
Bronaugh, Fannie	28
Bronaugh, Fanny	29
Bronaugh, John	29
Bronaugh, John & Hannah	80
Brooks, John	20
Brooks, Julia	20
Brown, Auscar	67
Brown, Clark	111
Brown, J. M. (Rev.)	22
Brown, J. W.	31
Brown, J. W. (Elder)	4, 8, 10
Brown, J. W. (Rev.)	1, 14, 17, 27
Brown, Martin	26
Browning, James	81
Bruce, Katie	93
Bruce, T. P.	93
Bryant, Esquire	52
Bryant, James	104
Buford, Bettie	52
Buford, Col.	52
Bullingsworth, Katie	72
Burnes, Fielding	116
Burnes, Mamie	107
Burnett, Mary	92
Burruss, Mr. (Rev.)	35
Burruss, P. J. (Elder)	48
Burt, James	52
Burt, John (Capt.)	52
Busey, Jacob T.	27
Byons, Letty D.	43
Bywaters, J. C.	6
Bywaters, J. O.	59
Bywaters, R. W.	81
Bywaters, William	59
Cain, Mary	91
Cain, Robert E.	52
Cain, Sue E.	106
Cain, Wm.	91
Call, Samuel (Mrs.)	100
Callahan, Kate	43
Calvert, William	35
Campbell, Mr. (Rev.)	111, 115
Campbell, W. C. (Rev.)	117
Canby, Geo.	111
Carman, J. L.	81
Carson, Robert (Mrs.)	67
Cartwright, C. M.	45
Cartwright, Geo.	101
Cartwright, I. P.	70
Caruthers, Mr. (Rev.)	35
Cary, May A.	5
Cary, Mollie	5
Casper, Ellington	32
Chance, D. A.	12
Chestnut, E.	63
Chestnut, Girard	63
Chestnut, Della L.	3
Chestnut, P.E.	3

Chestnut, Prettie Ellie 3	Cole, Martha E. 33
Chestnut, Wm. 43	Cole, Thomas J. 10
Chestnut, Wm. (Mr. & Mrs.) 3	Coleman, A. J. 7, 101
Chiles, (Judge) 2, 70	Coleman, A. J. (Mrs.) 101
Chinn, A. N. 41	Coleman, Cassie 101
Chinn, Cornelia 41	Coleman, H. C. 101
Chinn, Geo. W. 23	Coleman, Jane 101
Chinn, J. H. 107	Coleman, T. H. (Mrs.) 101
Chinn, P. W. 110	Coleman, Thomas H. 30
Christy, James 50	Collet, Abraham 21
Christy, Luanna 50	Collet, Sarah 21
Clay, Ida 99	Collins, Hattie 45, 85
Clay, J. (Rev.) 58, 109	Collins, John 7, 56, 85
Clay, Jeramiah (Rev.) 61	Collins, Mary E. 56
Clay, Jeremiah (Rev.) 31, 66	Collins, Myra 7
Clay, Thomas 99	Connor, W. S. (Rev.) 102
Clay, William 18	Coons, Thorton 77
Clay, Willie 58	Cooper John 38
Clay, Wm. 21	Cooper, Cornelius 39
Clemings, Charlotte T. 9	Cooper, Charity 102
Clemings, G. F. 9	Cooper, Eddie Oscar 38
Clemings, Janie 45	Cooper, Henry 102
Clemmings, G. F. 43	Cooper, Martha 38
Clemmings, Jennie 99	Cooper. Robert Edgar 102
Clifford, J. (Mr. & Mrs.) 71	Corbin, Melissa D. 32
Cober, Dink 52	**Cormack, J. L.** 68
Cockrill, Blanche 60	Couch, Dora M. 5
Cockrill, Cara E. 18	Couch, Margaret A. 87
Cockrill, Clint 101	Couch, William M. 86
Cockrill, Clinton 14	Couch, Wm. 5, 87
Cockrill, Grundy 78	Cox, Marcus Aurelus 21
Cockrill, Helen C. 18	Cox, W. G. 102
Cockrill, Lizzie 14	Cox, W. G. 70, 88
Cockrill, Mr & Mrs. F. G. 60	Creek, Jacob 60
Cockrill, W. F. 18	Creek, Virginia 60
Coffey, Catherine 39	Crobarger, George W. 22
Coffey, Dr. & Mrs. 101	Crockett, S. M. (Esquire) 81
Coffey, E. McD. 116	Crouch, Mr. (Rev.) 86
Coffey, Fred 39	Crouch, W. A. (Rev.) 107
Coffey, R. N. (Dr.) 39	Crowbarger, Cattie M. 61
Coffey, Sheriff 35	Curran, H. W. (Rev.) 32
Cole William 65	Currin, H. W. (Rev.) 15
Cole, David 65	Daniels, Mammie 117
Cole, David H. 86	Daniels, William 117
Cole, James 65	Darley, Josie 22
Cole, John R. 33	Darnall, Milton 11

Name	Page
Darnall, R. T.	11, 107
Darnall, R. T. (Mr. & Mrs.)	70
Darnell, Lee M.	22
Davidson, Fannie	2
Davis, E. J.	75
Davis, J. C.	32
Davis, Spicey	67
Davis, W. W.	32
Dean, Isaac	26
Dean, J. B. (Mrs.)	62
Dean, John B.	107
DeBard, Henry	42
DeBeery, William	13
Demasters, A. R.	78
Demoss, Sarah A.	81
Denton, Robert	110
Devlin, Brother	16
Devlin, Joseph (Rev.)	55, 60
Dibble, P. K. (Elder)	50
Dietz, Lou	48
Dillingham, Amanda	63
Dillingham, Elisha	70
Dillingham, John	70
Dohart, Prof.	82
Dougherty, Fannie	110
Douglas, A. T.	17
Ducoing, Emma S.	34
Dunagan, Sidney Jane	73
Duncan, Mrs.	72
Duncan, Annie	81
Duncan, John R.	81
Duncan, Ran.	109
Duncan. Isabella	81
Edgar, Mrs.	62
Edwards, Bell	38
Edwards, David R.	5
Ellifrit, R. T.	100
Ellifrit, Robert C.	100
Ellis, J. W. (Rev.)	99
Ellis, Mr. (Rev.)	38
Endicott, W. M.	88
Eskridge, Lucinda	37
Eskridge, T. K.	77
Estes, Alice	53
Estes, B. W.	53
Evans, Bam	22
Fackler, J. G. (Rev.)	113
Farra, John	94
Farra, John F.	95
Feeback, Francis A.	107
Fenloe, Thos. B.	91
Field, Clemmie	113, 114
Field, G. W.	26
Field, Jennie	113
Field, Julia	113
Field, Marshall	113
Field, William H.	113
Fields, Deede	68
Fields, G. W.	68
Figley, Mary E.	34
Figley, Wm.	43
Fisher, David S.	107
Fisher, Mary C.	107
Fisher, Mr.	95
Fitzgerald, O. P. (Rev.)	1
Flannery, James	67
Flannery, James F.	111
Flannery, Jas.	101
Flannery, John (Mrs.)	30
Flannery, John B.	40
Flannery, Mary L.	111
Fleshman, Wm.	106
Flishman, John H.	69
Flynn, Esquire	73
Flynn, M. A. (Esq.)	45
Foley, Catherine	71
Foote, George H.	1
Forbes, J. F.	85
Ford, Mattie	104
Ford, Wm.	33
Foreman, F. P. (Rev.)	5
Foster, Harry (Rev.)	83
Fox, James	37
Fox, Lucinda	102
Fox, William A.	37
Fox, Wm. A.	102
Fulton, Margaret	13
Fulton, William	13
Gabbert, Laura B.	68
Gaines, T. N. (Eld.)	72
Galbraith, Mary E.	2
Gaylord, (Prof)	70

Gaylord, F. G. 45, 54
Geary, E. R. (Rev.) 64
George, Mrs. 89
George, T. B. 89
Gibson, John 111
Gibson, Susan 111
Gilbert, Ben W. 45, 47
Gilbert, Cyrus P 8
Gilbert, Elma Ber 8
Gilbert, Mary 8
Gilbert, Thompson A. 48
Gilkeson, A. D. 97
Gittinger, James 36
Graves, Phebe 75
Gray, Henry 81
Greeg, Anna 62
Green, A. N. 93
Green, F. M. 101
Green, George D. 41
Green, Matilda 93
Green, William A. 89
Grimes, C. (Rev.) 2
Grimes, Lizzie 94
Grinestead, Miss 35
Guthrie, Elvira 87
Guthrie, John M. 87
Guthrie, Willie 101
Hall, Allen R. 10
Hall, Tinnie 110
Hamilton, James 63, 70
Hamilton, John 70
Hamilton, Lee 14
Hamilton, Samuel 14
Hamlin, Hattie 45
Hamm, Jacob S. 48
Handley, A M. I. 34
Handley, A. M. I. 38
Handley, A. M. J. 33
Handley, Father (Rev.) 108
Handley, James 33, 38
Handley, Sarah A. 33, 34, 38
Hardesty, Charles 24
Hardesty, Robt. 45
Harding, Chester (Gen.) 15
Hardwicke, J. B. (Rev.) 47
Hardwidke, J. B. (Rev.) 53

Harkrider, Miss 39
Harlan, Elizabeth 104
Harlan, Henry 104
Harlan, William C. 71
Harrington, Bettie 48
Harrington, Thomas 48
Harris, Charles 79
Hart, William 22
Harvel, James 7
Harvel, James (Mr. & Mrs.) 7
Harvey, John A. 99
Harvey, Mr. (Rev.) 48
Hatton, Clemmie 96, 99
Hatton, Esquire 34
Hawley, C. B. 45
Hawley, C. B. (Mr. & Mrs.) 101
Hawley, Mrs. 96
Hawley, Percey 101
Hawn, Mattie 30
Hayes, John T. 107
Helvey, James 100
Henry, Frankie 108
Henry, Thomas 108
Henry, Thos. (Capt.) 109
Herndon, S. W. 86
Herndon, Thomas 57
Herron, Laura 79
Higgason, A. E. (Elder) 58
Hill, Archibald 62
Hodges, Samuel 23
Hoeck, Fred 103
Hollingsworth, Mrs. 101
Holt, A. T. 44
Holt, J. M. (Dr.) 112
Holt, Jim (Dr.) 8
Home, Mahala Davis 83
Hon, Belle 11
Hon, Gertie 11
Hon, Issac 112
Hon, Nannie 22
Hon, T. L. 11
Horn, Alex 61
Hoy, Samuel 83
Hoy, Lydia 83
Hoy, May 83
Hudson, J. A. 66

Birth's, Death's and Marriages from the Platte City Missouri "Landmark"

Name	Page
Hudson, Miss	36
Hughes, A. W.	12
Hughes, John	31
Hughes, Sarah	31
Humphrey, Lizzie	117
Hunt, Charles	12
Hunt, Mr. [Coon?]	12
Hunt, Pheule	12
Hunter, Tat	81
Hurst, L. A.	43
Hurst, Thomas (Rev.)	34
Hurst, Thos. (Rev.)	43
Ireland, George	109
Ireland, James E.	109
Ivens, Ben	27
Jack, John W.	66
Jacks, C. J.	82
Jacks, M. S.	82
Jacks, Tilden Hendricks	82
Jamis, Joseph C.	62
Jenkins, Howel	25
Jenkins, J. W.	96
Jenkins, Thomas E.	25
Jenkins, Tom	105
Jenkins, William T.	25
Jenkins, W. T.	45
Jesse, Adaline	39
Jesse, James	35
Jesse, John	39
Jesse, Richard H.	39
Johnson, Alice	8
Johnson, Dora	10
Johnson, F. M. (Dr.)	10
Johnson, LeVerrier	108
Johnson, Paisley	61
Johnson, R. D. (Capt.)	8
Johnson, Richard M.	91
Johnson, Stephen	99
Johnston, Emma	32
Johnston, Georgia	32
Johnston, Mary	15
Jones, Charlotte	117
Jones, Frank	3
Jones, George T.	44
Jones, John	55
Jones, Mr.	91
Jones, Tommy (Uncle)	91
Jones, Vincent (Rev.)	61
Jones, W. P.	3
Justus, J. F.	39
Kearnes, Hannah Malinda	19
Keen, John P.	45
Keith, J. C. (Eld.)	106
Kendrick, Carroll (Elder)	25
Kerr, William S.	114
Kidwell, Ollie	73
Kimsey, Benjamin	60
Kimsey, Elizabeth Ann	72
Kimsey, Patsy	17
Kimsey, Thomas	17
Kimsey, W. H & E. A.	72
Kimsey, Wade H.	17
King, James A.	106
Kirch, Rosa	63
Kirtley, Phillip	11
Kirtley, Sue E.	11
Kitchen, Geo.	75
Kitchen, Lou	75
Kline, H. S.	35
Knopf, Victoria (Mrs.)	64
Kurtz, Charles B.	48
Kurtz, Chas. B.	101
Kurtz, Gracie	48
Kuykendall, Elizabeth	9
Kuykendall, John	9
Kuykendall, Katie	67
Lamar, Charles H.	30
Lamar, F.	109
Lamar, L. L.	109
Lampton, B. L.	68
Lampton, Eudalia T.	58
Lampton, Jennie	60, 65
Lampton, John	60, 65
Lampton, L. B.	76
Lampton, Logan B.	74
Lampton, Logan B. (Mr. & Mrs.)	76
Lampton, Sallie	76
Lampton. Beverly T.	76
Langley, Samuel	9
Lanter, Capt. Davis	67
Lanter, Sidney	24, 67
Lanter, Spicey	67

Lanter, Thomas	67
Lanzer, Henry	7
Lanzer, Jane	7
Larey, A. J.	35
Lattin, Eva	2
Lawerence, James	9
Layton, Perry M.	27
Layton, Sally	27
Leavel, Archibald T.	25
Leavel, Hayden T.	84
Leavel, Mollie	84
Lee, J. N. (Rev.)	30
Lee, Mattie	48
Lee, Stephen	48
Lewis, A. T. (Rev.)	81
Lewis, Cad (Rev.)	75
Lewis, Katie	3
Lewis, Malin	3
Lewis, Mr. (Rev.)	90
Lewis, Rosa	10
Lewis, William	56
Link, D. J.	115
Link, David	69
Link, David J.	68
Link, E. J. (Mr. & Mrs.)	65
Link, Eli	98, 108
Link, Jake	103
Link, Levi A.	108
Link, Matilda E.	68, 69
Littlejohn, James H.	12
Loan, Benjamin	91
Loan, Charles	91
Loan, Joseph W.	91
Loan, Richard	91
Loan, William	91
Logan, Amanda V.	45
Long, A. A.	88
Long, Benj. S.	92
Long, E. R.	48
Long, Garrard	116
Loveland, Helen	84
Lutes, Joseph P.	53
Lutes, Neal	105
Lutes, Nealy	101
Luty, J. R.	38
MacIntosh, Annie (Mrs.)	97
Magers, Emma	45
Magers, Frederick	45
Magers, Lewis C.	61
Malott, Alice	45
Mann, Henry C.	50
Marshall, A. G.	116
Marshall, Amos G.	14
Marshall, burying ground	93
Marshall, Celia W.	99
Marshall, Clemmie	113
Marshall, Delia	44
Marshall, Erle	116
Marshall, Frederick	97, 113, 114
Marshall, Jennie	96
Marshall, M. A.	89, 104
Marshall, Mary E. (Mrs.)	116
Marshall, Mrs.	28
Martin, George	40
Mason, George	45, 70, 99
Mason, John	116
Mason, Laura	15
Mason, R. F.	15
Mattox, Dock	106
Maupin, J. H. (daughter)	101
May, B. L.	89
Mayo, G. W. (Rev.)	107
Mayo, H. J.	103
Mayo, Mary E.	103
Mayo, R. J.	103
Mayo, Richard	15
Mayo, Washington	106
McAfee, Prof.	97
McAffee, George	98
McCall, Mrs.	18
McClary, J. B. (Eld.)	56
McClary, J. B. (Elder)	7, 10
McClary, J. H. (Elder)	9
McCleary, J. B. (Elder)	63
McCleary, J. B. (Rev.)	99
McCleery, J. B. (Elder)	22
McComas, Hiram	117
McCord, James (Capt.)	10
McCormack, Joseph	40
McEowen, Julia	59
McFarland, H.	86
McFarland, Sue B.	86

Birth's, Death's and Marriages from the Platte City Missouri "Landmark"

Name	Page
McGeorge, William	68
Mcgeorge, Wm	81
McKee, Joseph	72
McKinnis, Laura	84
McKinnis, Lizzie E.	66
McKinnis, W. C.	84
McMichael, J. W.	46
McNemar, B. F.	26
McNemar, Bettie C.	62
McPike, William H.	90
McVey, F. M.	117
Meade, Arthur G.	101
Meade, Harry Ross	89
Meade, Henry	89
Meade, Henry (Mrs.)	101
Meade, Myra	89
Meades, Henry (Rev.)	100
Merchant, Eliza	60
Mercy, George R.	60
Merryman, Joseph E.	54
Meyer, Lou	42
Meyer, Randolph	42
Middleton, Mary	103
Middleton, Robt.	103
Middleton, W. M.	95
Miller, A.	19
Miller, Anderson	49
Miller, Emm	17
Miller, Florence	45
Miller, Hugh	3
Miller, Huston	3
Miller, James	45
Miller, Jesse	49
Miller, John	17
Miller, M. M.	83
Miller, Mary	48, 49
Miller, Mary A. E.	60
Miller, W. J.	83
Miller's, Elliott J.	41
Minor, Anna	62
Minor, William E.	62
Minter, Carrie	32
Montague, Benjamin	104
Monzey, Joseph	61
Moody, Isaac N.	115
Moore, Charles	81
Moore, J.	86
Moore, Miss Ella	1
Morgan, L. M.	106
Morgan, Silas D.	78
Morgan, Sudie	8
Morin, Jesse	93
Morin, Jesse, (Maj.)	31
Morin, Jessie (Mrs.)	31
Morin, John	63, 96
Morin, Zerelda V.	31
Morris, James	45
Morrow, Ellen S.	84
Morrow, William	84
Morton, Eleanor L.	14
Morton, J. F. (Dr.)	14
Morton, Richard	14
Murdock, Bettie	104
Murdock, C. T.	45
Murdock, Robert	32
Murley, Fannie	27
Murray, Willie	12
Nash, Mrs.	10
Naylor, (Graveyard)	74
Naylor, Ignatius	58
Naylor, Northcut Washington	19
Nelson,, W. F.	17
Newman Mr. (Rev.)	39
Newman, M. David	115
Nicol, David	88
Noland, John W.	81
Noll, Dora	48
Norton, E. H	104
Norton, E. H.	113
Norton, E.H.	1
Norton, K. H.	97
Norton, Maggie	96
Nowland, James Henry	73
Oelschlager, Frederic H.	46
Oelschlager, Mrs.	46
Ohlschlager, F. H.	71
Oldham, Annie	70
Oldham, Billy	101
Oldham, Billy (Mrs.)	101
Oldham, F. M.	70
Oldham, Hallie E.	30
Oldham, Mary E.	117

Oldham, Mollie E. 117	Pence, Edward 87
Oldham, W. O. 94	Pendleton, David E. 4
Oldham, W. O. (Mr. & Mrs.) 70	Pendleton, Felix 15, 16
Olds, Mr. 41	Penhallegon, (Rev.) 96
Oleschlager, F. H. 43	Penhallegon, W. H. (Rev.) 104, 115
Oleschlager, Mrs. 43	Perrin, Mary 16
Oliver, Ann 73	Perrin, Wm. F. 16
Oliver, Fannie 77	Perry, America R. 63
Oliver, Helen M. 88	Perry, Ben 45
Oliver, L. T. 46, 88	Perry, Ben E. 79
Oliver, William E. 73	Perry, Charles E. 63
Owen, Dorcas H. 78	Perry, Ruth Ann 79
Owens, Alfred (Mrs.) 79	Perry. Deborah 79
Owens, Eli 103	Peters, John R. 20
Owens, Giles 78	Peters, Robt. 86
Owens, Harvey 5	Phelps, Lydia... 4
Owens, Judge 78	Phillips, Mattie 77
Owens, Madison 5	Phillips, Timothy 34
Parish, Isaac O. (Mrs.) 14	Pitt, Lula 70
Park, Anna B. 79	Poland, J. H. (Rev) 8
Park, Clay (Hon.) 47	Porter, Georgia A. 8
Park, J.J. 107	Powell, Annette Jackson 54
Park, Jefferson J. and Mattie 77	Powell, E. C. 44
Park, John W. 80	Powell, Elijah C. 54, 56
Park, Lida 3	Powell, N. J. 54
Park, Lida F. 63	Prather, A. B. 51
Park, Maggie E. 101	Prather, Jas. 51
Park, Mattie 20	Price, Jas A. 51
Park, Sidney 85	Price, John M. 53
Park, Simpson 20, 63, 70	Price, Mollie F. 53
Park, T. W. 101	Price, Ross (Mrs.) 51
Park, Willie C. 77	Price, Tho. F. 51
Park, Zon 101	Proctor, (Elder) 87
Parr, Georgia E. 1	Proctor, A. (Elder) 117
Parrish, Lou 66	Pullins, Charles W. 16
Parrish, T. L. 92	Pullins, Julia 41
Parrott, Jo 45	Pullins, William 16
Patterson, Prof. 28	Pumphrey, Joseph H. 61
Patton, Mollie 106	Pumphrey, Joshua 40
Patton, Sadie 106	Purrin, (Abe & Flora) 74
Patton, Thomas 106	Purrin, Tempie 74
Paxton, Messrs. 96	Quinn, Thomas 44
Paxton, Phebe 96	Racey, Jane 107
Payne, Katie 3	Ratliff, James 69
Payton, Ellen 88	Ratliff, Matilda 69
Pemberton, Richard 73	Redman, C. C. 1

Birth's, Death's and Marriages from the Platte City Missouri "Landmark"

Name	Page
Reed, Mary D.	35
Rees, Richard R.	49
Reneau, Sue	78
Reneau, Sue D. (Mrs.)	78
Renfro, (Rev.)	19
Reynolds, J. T.	107
Richardson, Emma (Mrs.)	115
Richardson, Noble	98
Ridenbaugh, William	4
Ringo, Ella	97
Ringo, J. W. (Dr.)	97
Rixey, W. W.	45
Roberts, George	90
Robertson, Robert I.	23
Robertson, Sallie	23
Robinson, Georgie M.	7
Robinson, John D.	117
Rogers, Dora	86
Rogers, Dora M.	87
Rogers, J.C. (Dr.)	5
Rogers, Thos B.	1
Rogers, W. C. (Elder)	68, 103
Roney, W. H. (Judge)	99
Root, Oren (Rev.)	62
Rose, R. R.	35
Rose, Robt.	73
Russell, Ryland	51
Ryan, Catherine	18
Ryan, John	18
Sandusky, Mattie	2
Sandusky, S. D.	2
Schmuttie, August	42
Schneider, Hartman	99
Searce, Dolly	43
Searcy, Fannie	35
Searcy, Nat	35
Settle, C. H.	48, 49
Settle, Jesse B.	48
Shanks, William B.	32
Shepard, Paul	72
Sherwood, Sue	61
Shopse?, B. F.	26
Shortridge, Dr.	65
Shortridge, John	13
Shortridge, W. T.	60
Shouse, Lewis	51
Siler, Lewis	98
Silvey, James M.	79
Silvey, Lucy G.	79
Silvey, James M.	79
Simmons, Joel	99
Simmons, Mary	99
Simpson, Jennie	54
Simpson, Preston	54
Singleton, Charles B.	53
Singleton, Wm. A.	54
Sloan,	83
Sloan, Allen	83, 84, 97
Sloan, David	54
Sloan, Mahala	83
Sloan, Mrs.	83
Sloan, William	84
Slone, Mary F.	97
Smith	71
Smith, A. F. (Elder)	77
Smith, A. F. (Eld.)	71, 79
Smith, A. F. (Elder)	85, 93, 104, 108, 109, 110, 116, 117
Smith, A. G. (Esquire)	73
Smith, A. T.	94
Smith, Alex.	12
Smith, R. Bunyan	113
Snail, James B.	24
Snail, Mr.	23
Snyder, Charles	67
Somerville, John	64
Soper, W. B.	81
Sowder, Lucy C.	65
Spencer, William	34
Spicer, Hiram	114
Spicer, Martha E.	113
Spratt, Edgar	103
Spratt, Esquire	104
Spratt, G. B.	12
Spratt, John A.	85
Spratt, John W.	43
Spratt, Sarah E.	85
Stallard, D. R.	81
Stallard, Isabella	109
Stallard, Luther	117
Stallard, Marcellus	81, 109
Starks, Price	14

Starks, Price (Mrs.)	14	Thomas, Wm. H. (Elder)	6
Steele, Oliver	67	Thomas, T. L.	96
Stephens, John H.	84	Thompson, G. W.	12
Stewart	78	Thompson, Lizzie	12
Stewart, Jennie	78	Thompson, N. A.	12
Stewart, Paulina	22	Thompson, Robt.	12
Stitt, Mary	82	Timberlake, John	112
Stitt, W.E.	41	Timberlake, Nicholas	112
Stitt, Watson. B.	82	Timberlake, Obediah	74
Stitt, William	82	Tinder, Dudley	86
Story, Ella	48	Tinder, Larkin E.	117
Story, Geo S.	48	Tinder, Millie	86
Stout, Charles	101	Todd, (Widow)	17
Stout, Mr. & Mrs.	101	Todd, A. H.	8
Summers, J. C.	116	Todd, Eliza	17
Summers, W. J.	116	Todd, Frank F.	78
Sutherland, J. C.	8	Todd, Hugh B.	80
Sutton, Carrie	24	Todd, Lucy	8
Swain, Bettie	91	Todd, M. L. (Capt.)	6
Swain, John R.	91	Todd, Rufus H.	2
Swain, Messrs.	96	Tribble, Elizabeth (Mrs.)	78
Swearenger, Venetia	1	Unknown, George (Rev.)	56
Sweeney, Dr. Loren	7	Unknown,, John	17
Synnamon, James	74	Uttinger, (Family)	52
Synnamon, Jane	74	Uttinger, Missouri	52
Synnamon, Lizzie Henderson	74	Vance, Jefferson	43
Tate, James	21	**Vandeventer, C. I. (Rev.)**	102
Tate, Jennie	21	Vierheilig, George	1
Tatman, Wm.	41	Wade, John W.	60
Taylor, [Jille] F.	63	Wade, Susan H.	60
Taylor, C. H.	63	Walker, Dr.	51
Taylor, Charles W.	89	Walker, John Churchwell	110
Taylor, J. Z. (Elder)	51	Walker, Martha (Patsey)	51
Teegarden, Luther	68	Walker, Perry	51
Thatcher, ??	43	Wallace, H. B.	84
Thatcher, Daniel	43	Wallace, James	10
Thatcher, John	72, 103, 114	Wallace. Dr.	83
Thatcher, Joseph	110	Waller, B. (Elder)	23, 103
Thatcher, Sarah	114	Waller, B. (Rev.)	110, 115
Thatcher, Sibbie	103	Waller, Brother	16
Thelkeld, M. E.	97	Waller, Elder	35
Thomas, Probasco (Esq.)	106	Waller, Fountain	15
Thomas, Richard (Elder)	24	Waller, J. W. (Elder)	3
Thomas, T. L.	45, 99, 108	Waller, Joseph (Elder)	2, 12
Thomas, W. H. (Elder)	40	Waller, Joseph W. (Elder)	5
Thomas, W. H. (Rev.)	48, 49	Waller, Kendrick	110

Name	Page	Name	Page
Waller, R. B. (Rev.)	43	Williams, William W.	95
Walters, Miss	1	Willis, Drury	71
Walters, Mr.	1	Willis, M. J.	71
Warner, George A.	50	Wills, Archibald	112
Warren, Annie	61	Wills, W. R. (Mr. & Mrs.)	100
Weldon, R. S.	19	Wilson, Ida	12
Wenfield, A. R. (Rev.)	66	Wilson, Martha	98
White, James	111	Wilson, Mary E.	1
White, Jas.	89	Winn, Annie	109
White, John C.	97	Wood, John	43
White, Mollie	89	Wood, Virgil	35
White, W. P.	107	Wood, William	89
Whitlock. Preston	13	Woods, Kemp M, (Jr)	75
Wigglesworth, Lillie M.	75	Woods, Mr.	75
Wilkerson, James C.	45	Woods, Walter N.	58
Wilkinson, Nathaniel	4	Woodson, Mary	33
Williams, (Elder)	25	Woodward, Rev.	30
Williams, America	86	Worth, Mr. (Rev.)	51
Williams, Bettie	86	Wyatt, Elder	62
Williams, Elder	41	Wyatt, J. J. (Elder)	89
Williams, Elisha	86	Yates, Jno O.	77
Williams, Frank	86	Yocum, Frank	98
Williams, L. S. (Mrs.)	116	Zarn, Jno.	84
Williams, Mary F.	95	Zarn, John	101
Williams, W. H.	30	Zarn, Johnny N.	84
Williams, W. H. (Eld.)	22	Ziswyler, P. (Rev.)	45
Williams, W. H. (Elder)	15, 32, 43, 50, 54		

www.ingramcontent.com/pod-product-compliance
Lightning Source LLC
Chambersburg PA
CBHW081134170426
43197CB00017B/2860